BOOK #12   "THE FIGHT FOR THE..."

TUTTLE TWINS

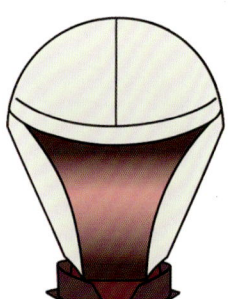

TUTTLE TWINS ● **BOOK #12** ● **First Printing Nov 2022**
Published by: Tuttle Twins Show, llc © 2022, all rights reserved
Printed by: Shyft Global

Showrunner/Director/Writer: Daniel Harmon
Writers: Jonny Vance, Kellen Erskine, Natalie Madsen

Graphic Novel Art Director: Jared Sampson
Interior Layouts, Design, FX, and Lettering by:
Ben Woolston, Jay Layne, Brooke Hancock, Jonathan Castro, Kenyon Davis, Nelson Quintero
Front Cover Design: Scott Brooks, Ben Woolston
Editor: Becky Ross Michael

All artistic representations of prominent characters featured herein and all likenesses are trademarks of Tuttle Twins Show, LLC unless otherwise noted. No part of this publication may be reproduced or transmitted in any form or by any means without the express written permission of Tuttle Twins Show, LLC. This print media is a reproduction and interpretation of the tv series "TUTTLE TWINS" and falls under appropriate copyrights to the intellectual properties of all parties involved. All artwork created is officially licensed.
For more information please contact admin@tuttletwins.tv.

WWW.TUTTLETWINS.TV   @TUTTLETWINSTV

ONE MINUTE EARLIER

ONE MINUTE LATER

IS THIS BECAUSE OF MY HATE MAIL TO THE IRS? I DIDN'T EVEN CURSE THIS TIME!

WHAT? NO. WE'RE FROM A NEW BRANCH OF GOVERNMENT, THE *FREEDOM AND REGULATION TEAM.*

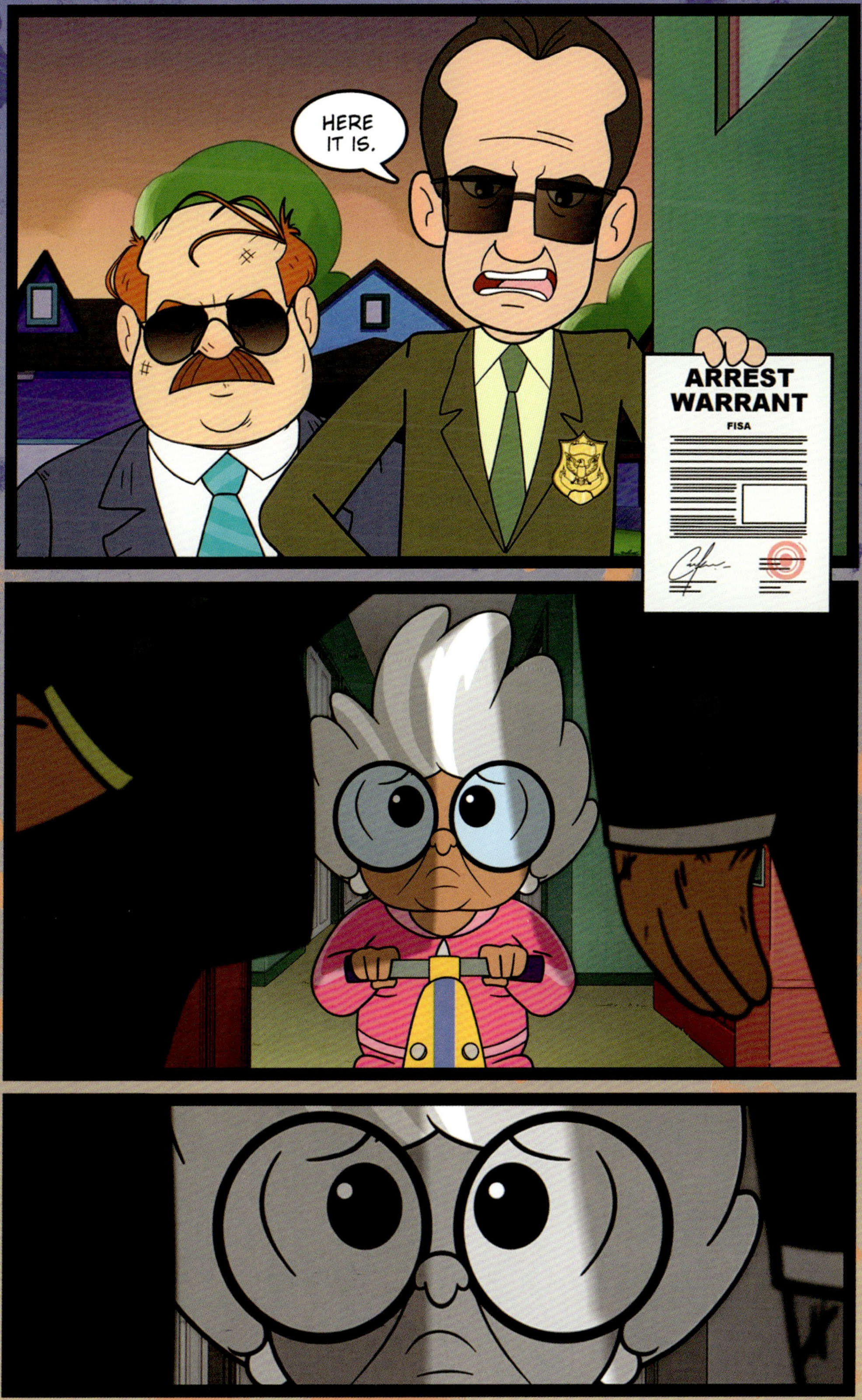

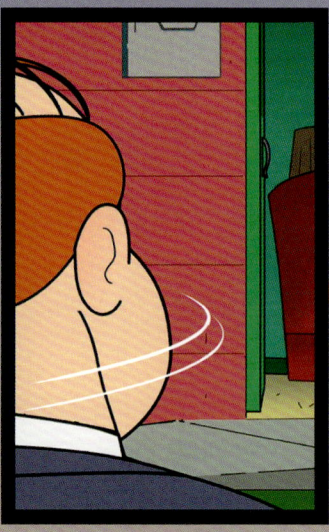

FINALLY, TIME TO SEIZE THAT WHEELCHAIR.

RRIIIP!
RRIIIP!

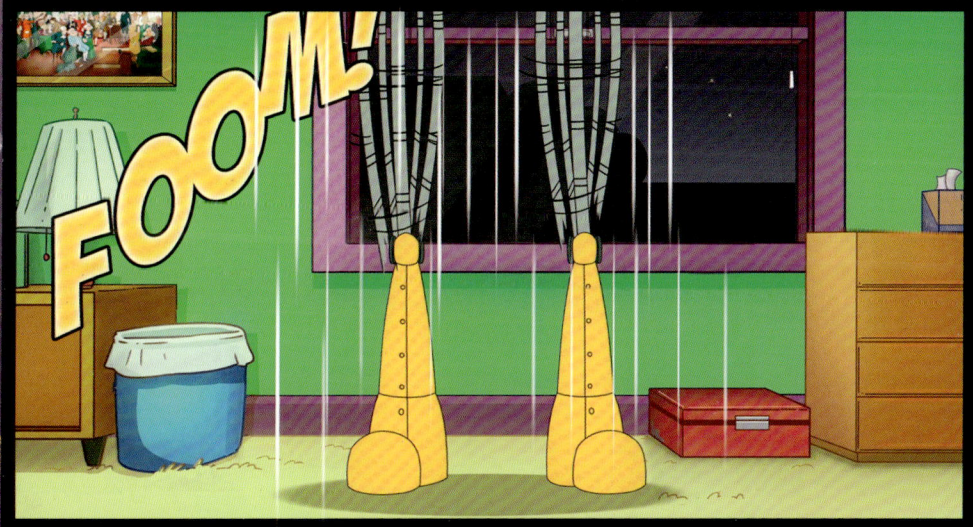

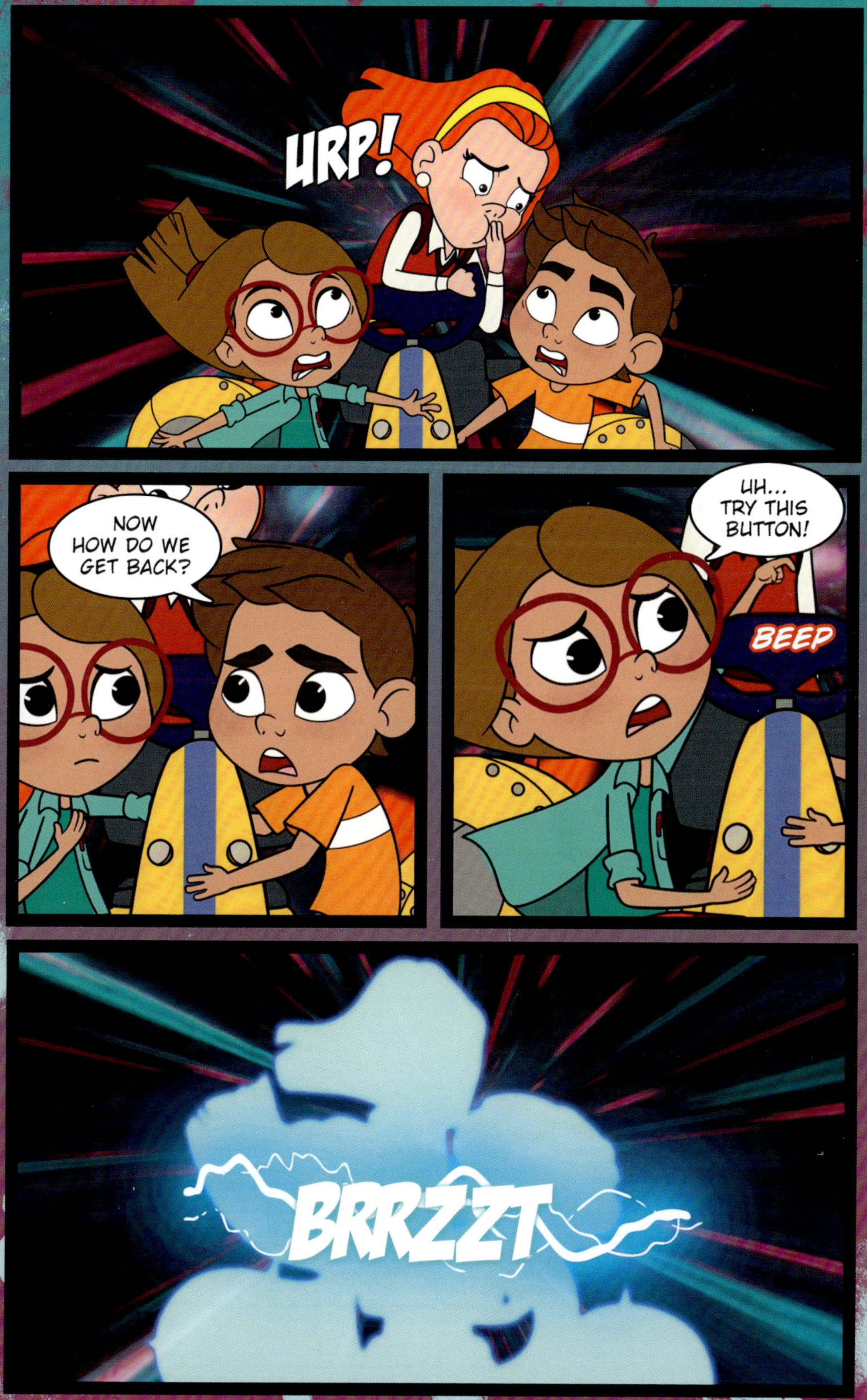
URP!
NOW HOW DO WE GET BACK?
UH... TRY THIS BUTTON!
BEEP
BRRZZT

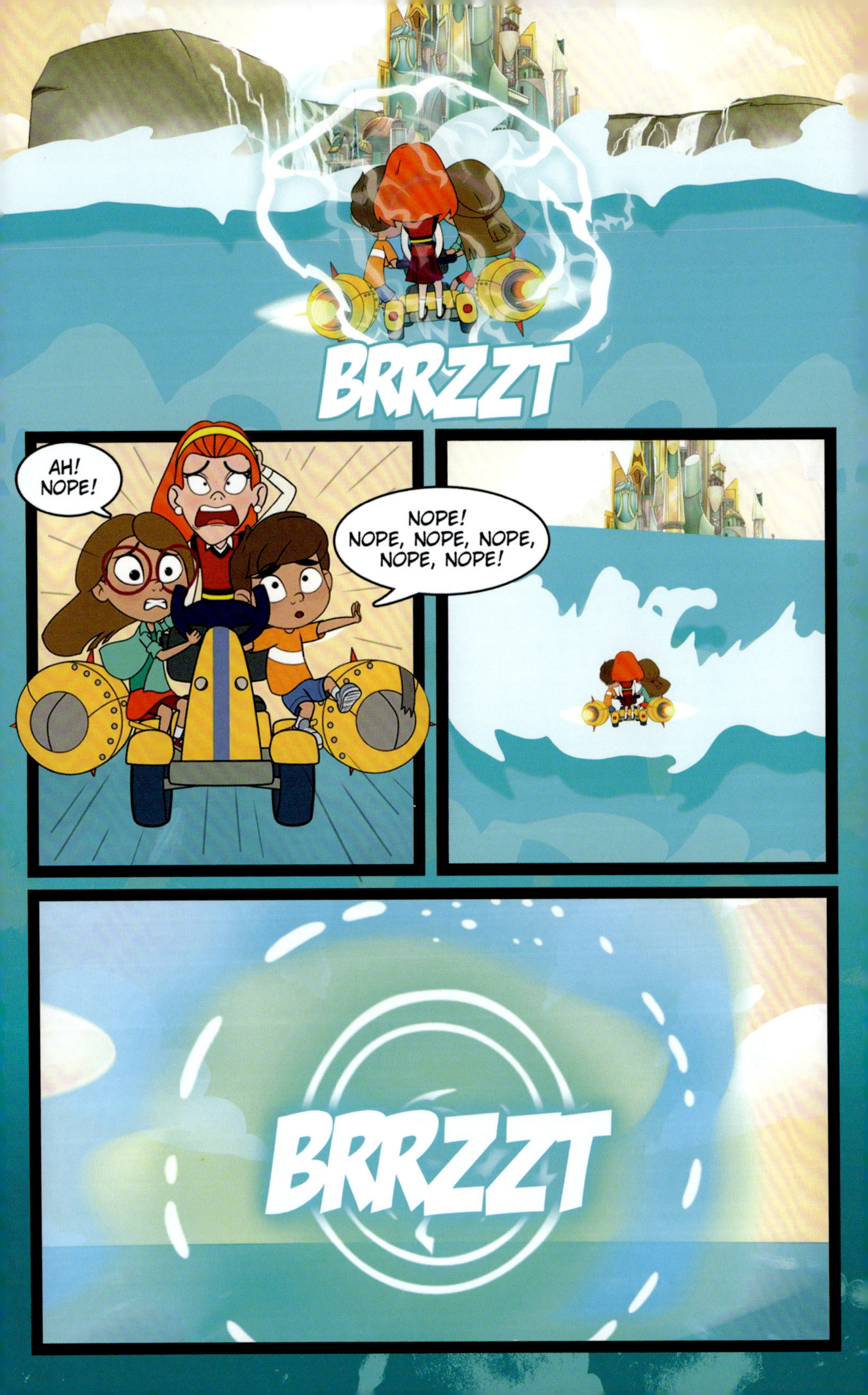
BRRZZT
AH! NOPE!
NOPE! NOPE, NOPE, NOPE, NOPE, NOPE!
BRRZZT

"THERE THEY ARE, GET 'EM!"

"AH! NOPE!"

BRRZZT

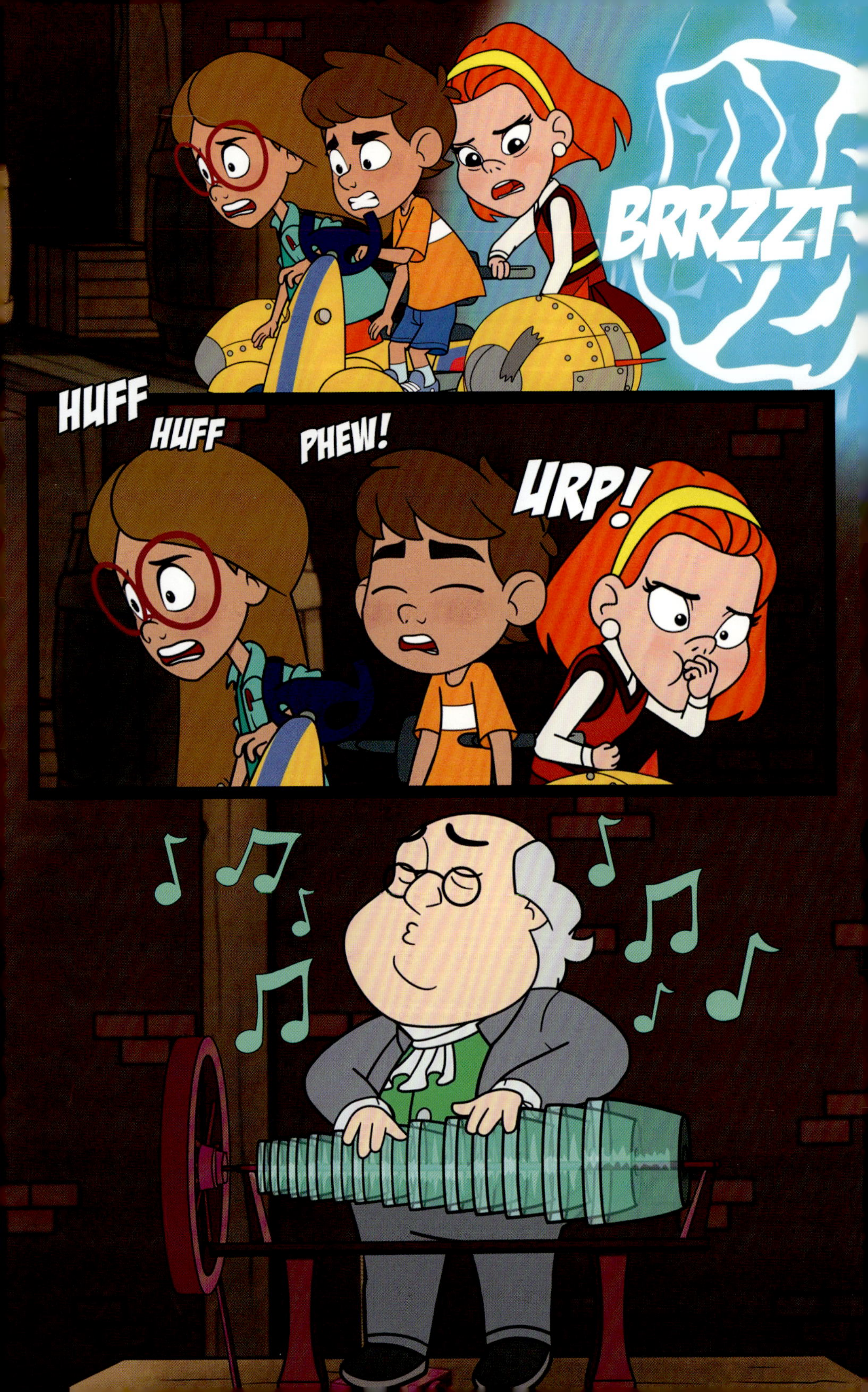
BRRZZT
HUFF
HUFF
PHEW!
URP!

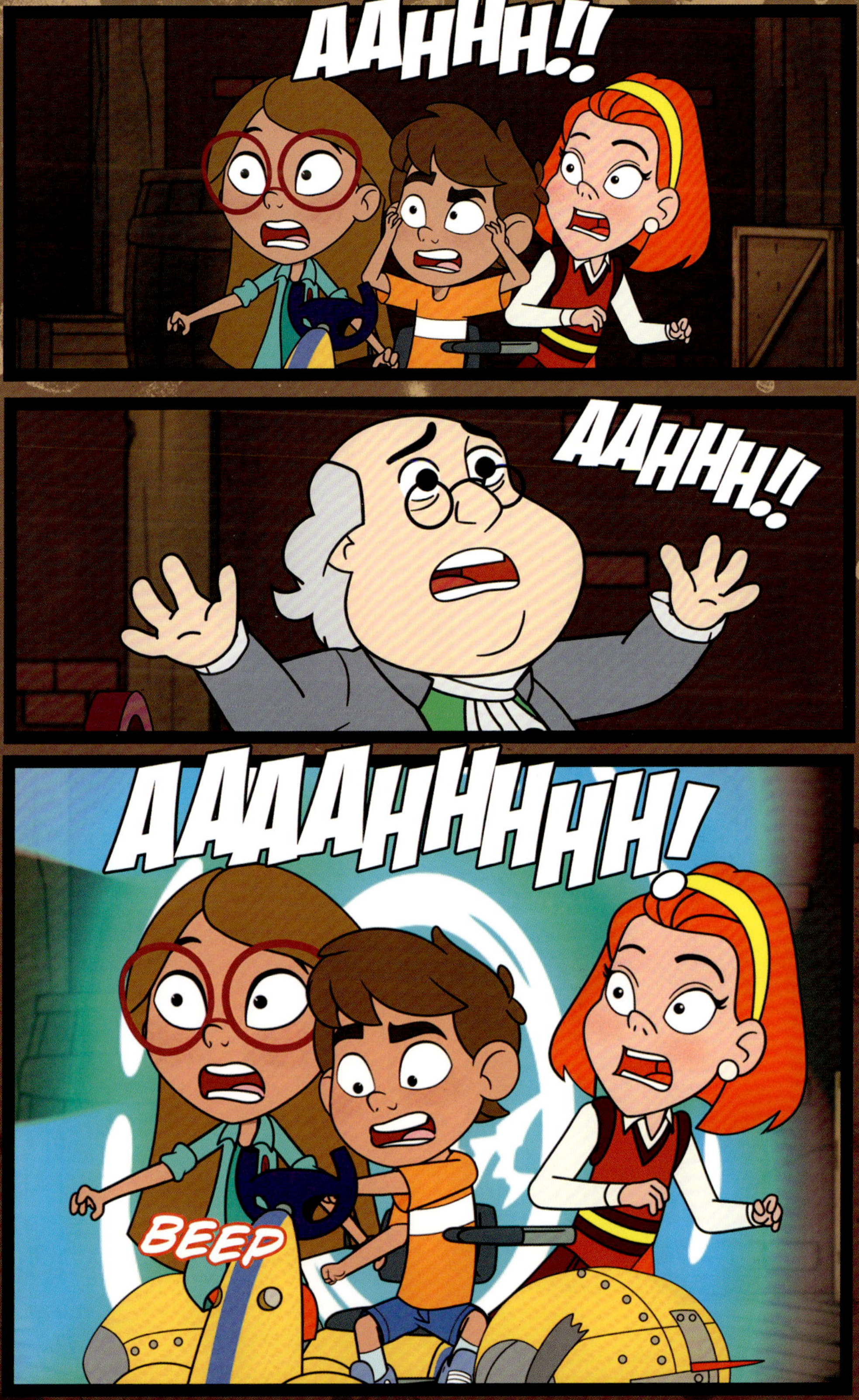
AAHHH!!
AAHHH!!
AAAAHHHHHH!
BEEP

THAT BIG WEIRD HEAD...
BRRRZZTT
PHEW, OKAY.. KARINNE! YOU CAN'T TELL ANYONE ABOUT THIS!
WHY NOT? IS IT *ILLEGAL?*
NO! I DON'T KNOW, MAYBE? UH... DOES THAT MEAN WE'RE ACCOMPLICES?!
COOL!

"NOT COOL, ETHAN! BUT... SOMETIMES IT'S OKAY TO CIVILLY DISOBEY."

"AND... WE'VE LEARNED SO MUCH BY HANGING OUT WITH OUR GRANDMA, WE DON'T WANT TO LOSE IT! JUST THINK OF YOU AND YOUR OWN GRANDMOTHER!"

SWEAR ALLEGIANCE TO THE KGB OR GET ME A SWITCH!

FLOP WAAAA!

LISTEN.

I CAN MAKE THIS WHOLE THING GO AWAY...

IF YOU MAKE ME KIDZ CLUB PRESIDENT AGAIN AND STOP GOING ON ADVENTURES WITH YOUR GRANDMA!

WHY DO YOU CARE ABOUT OUR ADVENTURES WITH OUR GRANDMA?

BECAUSE I'M LOSING CONTROL!

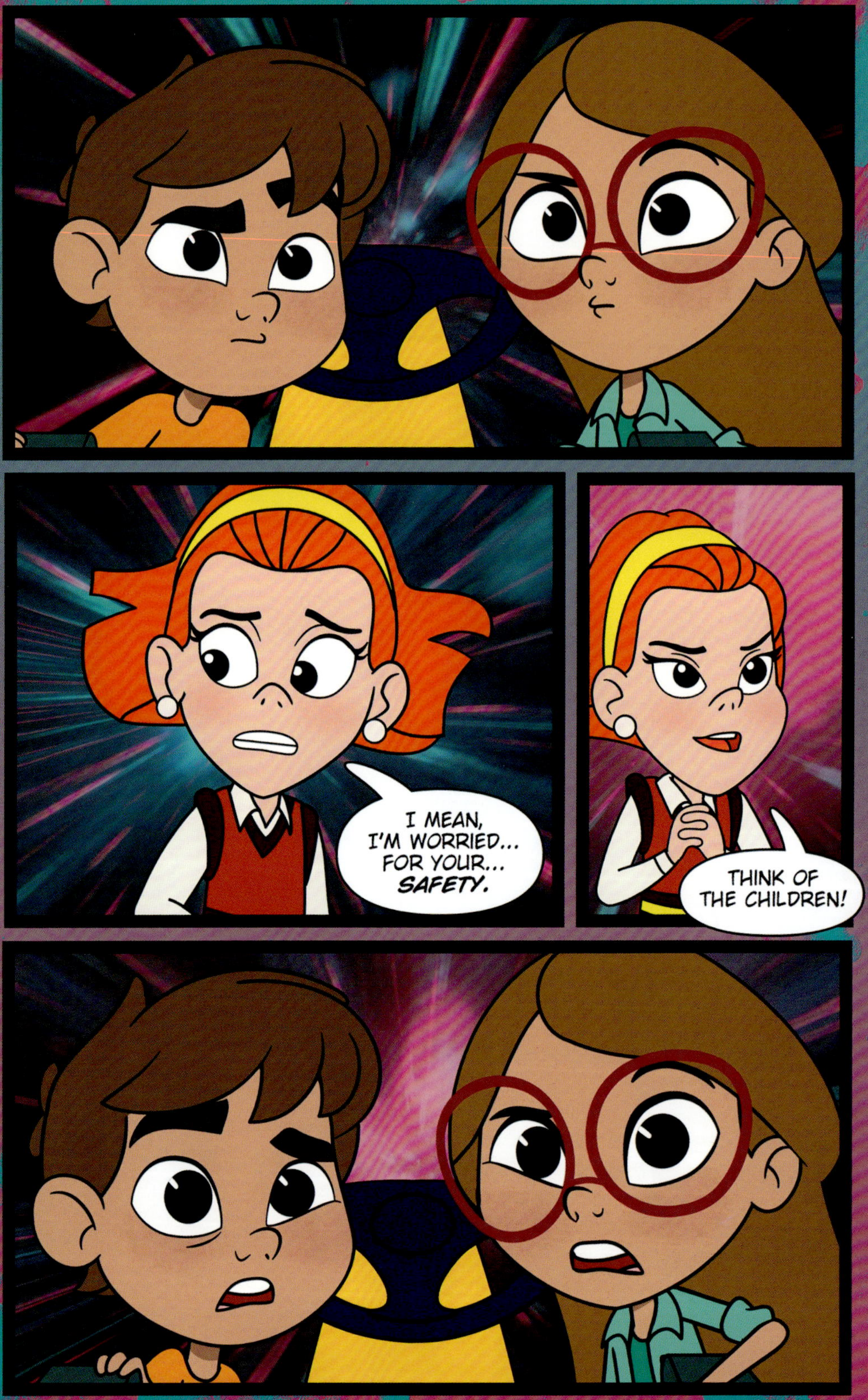
I MEAN, I'M WORRIED... FOR YOUR... SAFETY.
THINK OF THE CHILDREN!

I DON'T KNOW WHY IT'S THIS HARD OF A DECISION!
MAYBE THIS WILL HELP.
DEET
ZRRRM
Things the twins must NEVER know!

FEBRUARY 10, 3000

BUT, SHE SAID THAT GOING TO THE FUTURE WAS FORBIDDEN!
DOESN'T SEEM SO TRUSTWORTHY NOW, DOES SHE?
BEEP
BRRZZZ

HERE'S THE PLAN GRANDMA! WE CAN DO THIS THE EASY WAY...
OR WE CAN DO THIS THE HARD WAY.
GRRRR
WHAT IS THIS, BAD COP, WORSE COP?

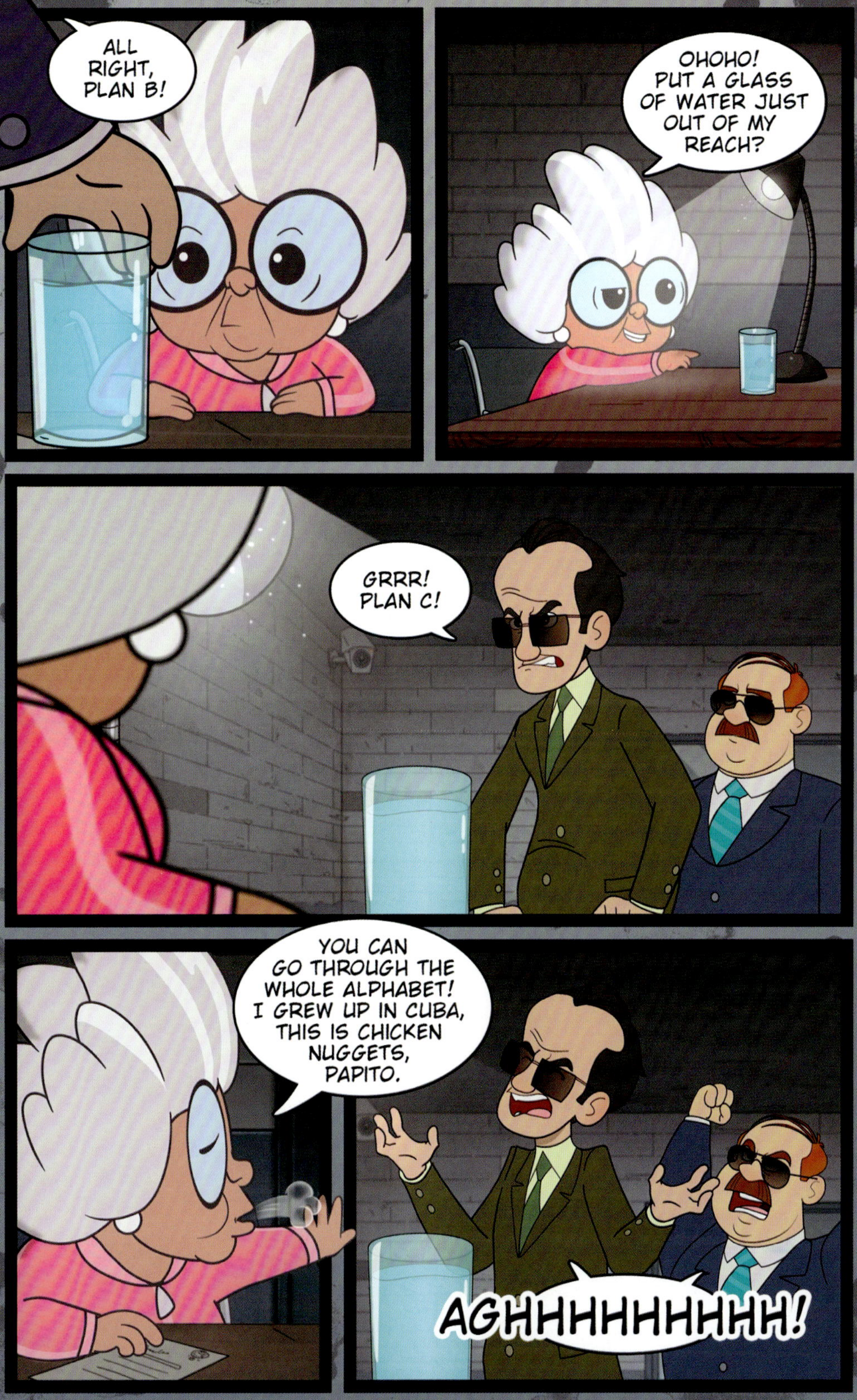
ALL RIGHT, PLAN B!
OHOHO! PUT A GLASS OF WATER JUST OUT OF MY REACH?
GRRR! PLAN C!
YOU CAN GO THROUGH THE WHOLE ALPHABET! I GREW UP IN CUBA, THIS IS CHICKEN NUGGETS, PAPITO.
AGHHHHHHHHH!

AAAAAAHHH!!
BRRZZT

POOF!

HEY, LOOK!
THE FUTTTURRRE!

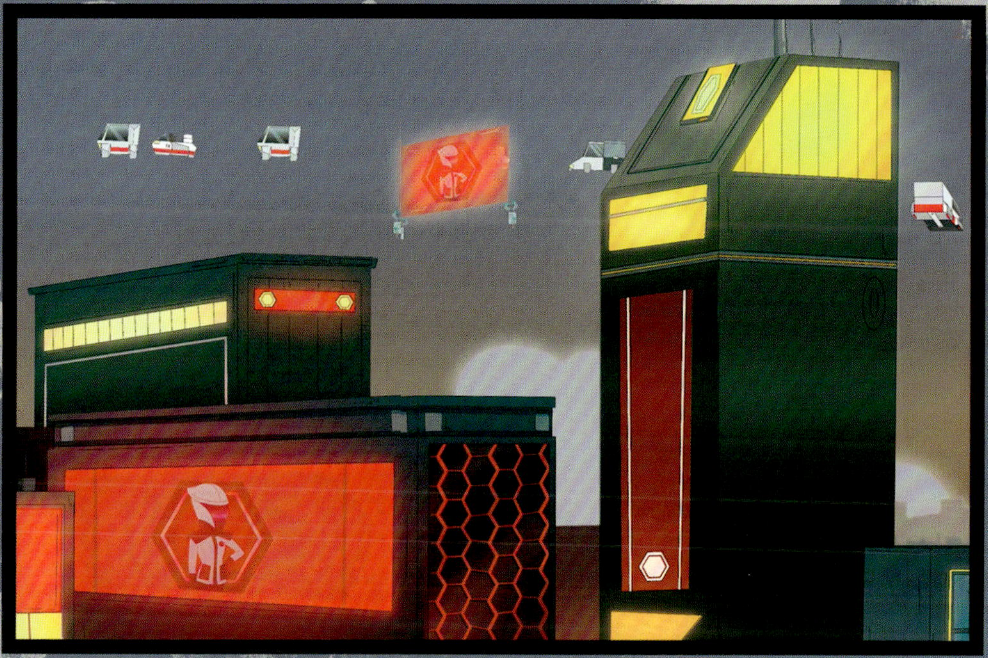
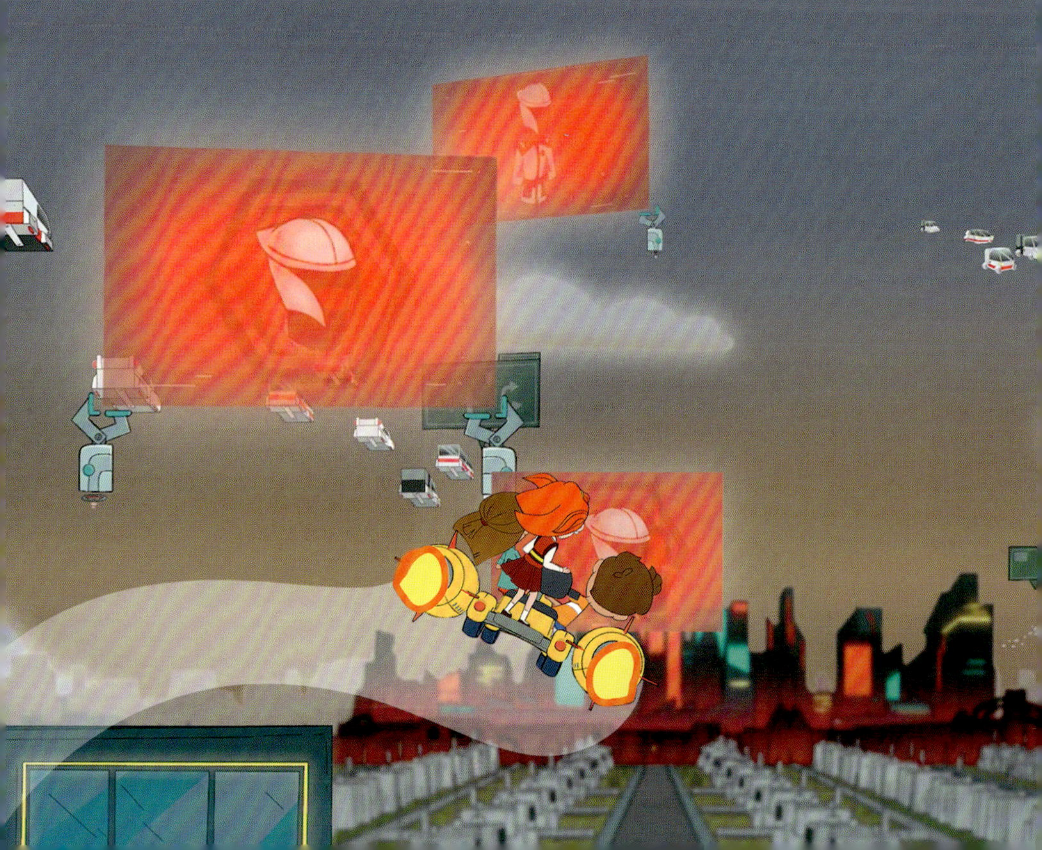

ZZTZTZT

AAAAAHHHHHHH!!

CRASH!

BEEP

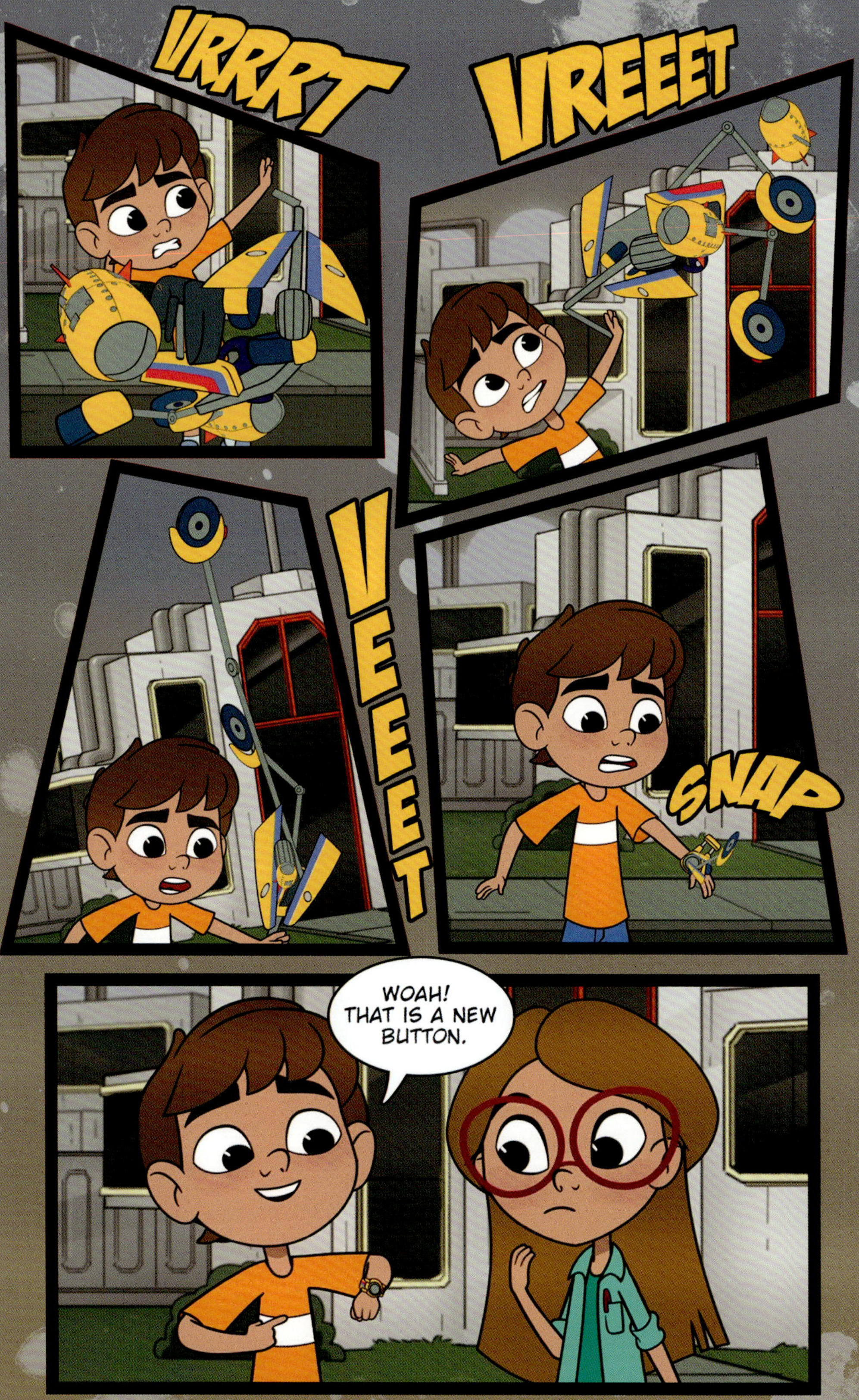
VRRRT
VREEET
VEEEET
SNAP
WOAH! THAT IS A NEW BUTTON.

WHAT IF WE HAD STILL BEEN ON IT!?
GOOD JOB! KEEP IT UP! YOUR PACE IS FASTER THAN AVERAGE!
TEAMWORK!
CLAP!
TOSS
BONK!
GOOD AIM!

THE FUTURE IS BEAUTIFUL!
WHAT DID I TELL YOU?
HOW IS THIS POSSIBLE?
WERE YOU BORN IN A 21ST CENTURY HOSPITAL? WATCH THE DAILY NEWS, SILLY.
HA! HA! HA!
SLAP
DING!

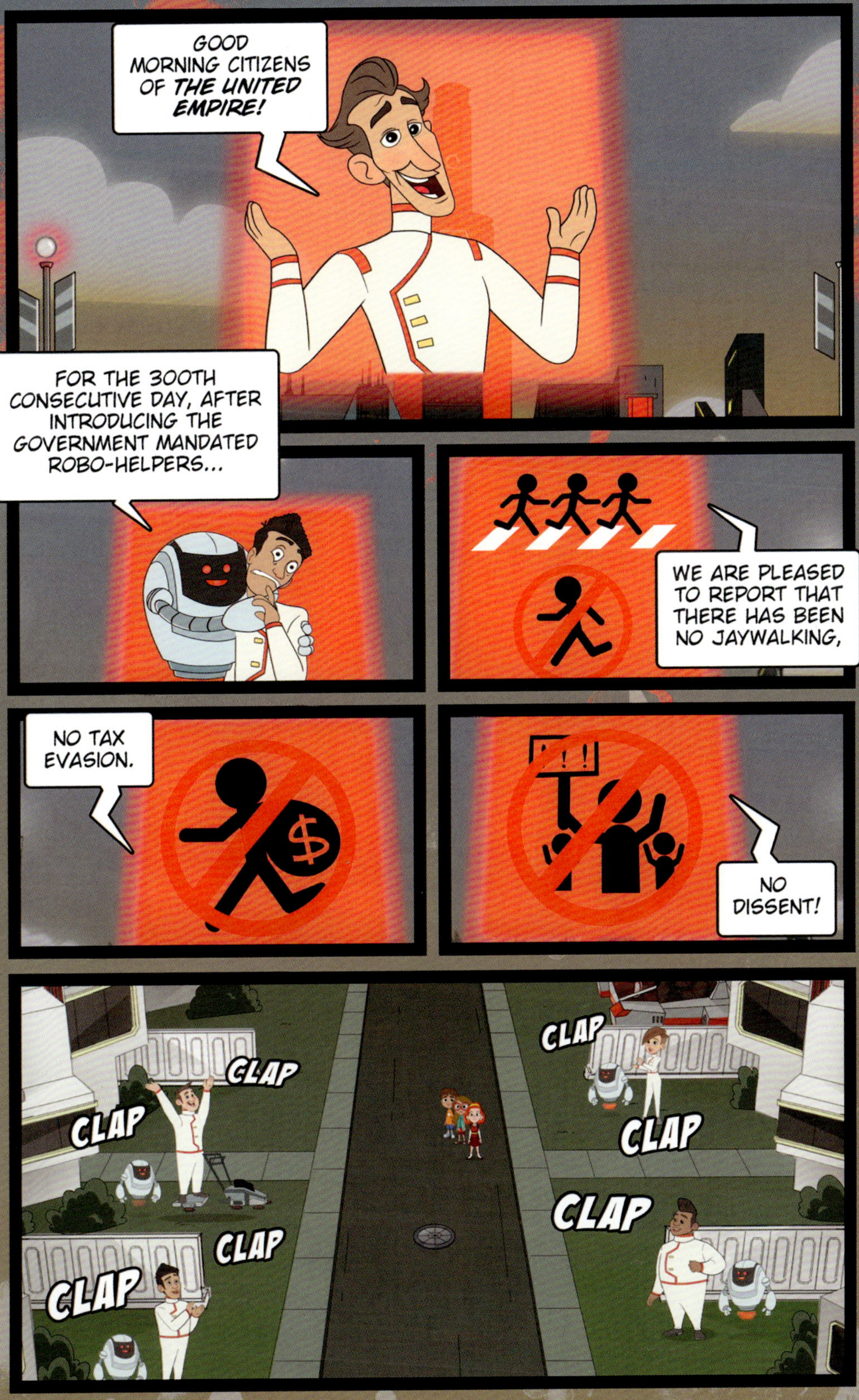

IN OTHER NEWS,
THE BENEVOLENT LEADER HAS INTRODUCED A NEW EXECUTIVE ORDER...
GIVING EVERYONE FREE MANDATED MUFFINS ON MONDAYS!
MUFFIN MONDAY!
IT IS ALSO NOW ILLEGAL FOR ANYONE ELSE TO SELL MUFFINS.
GASP!
MUFFIN 4 SALE!
OH COME ON!
FLIP!

FIRST CROISSANTS, NOW MUFFINS! HOW AM I SUPPOSED TO MAKE A LIVING BAKING STUFF?
WAH!!
YOINK
THAT WAS WEIRD.
PSSST- DOWN HERE, SMALL HUMANS.

I CAN SAVE YOU!

SAVE US? FROM WHAT? THE BEAUTIFUL FUTURE BUILT BY A BEAUTIFUL ALL POWERFUL GOVERNMENT? NO THANKS!

THOSE KIDS ARE LOITERING!

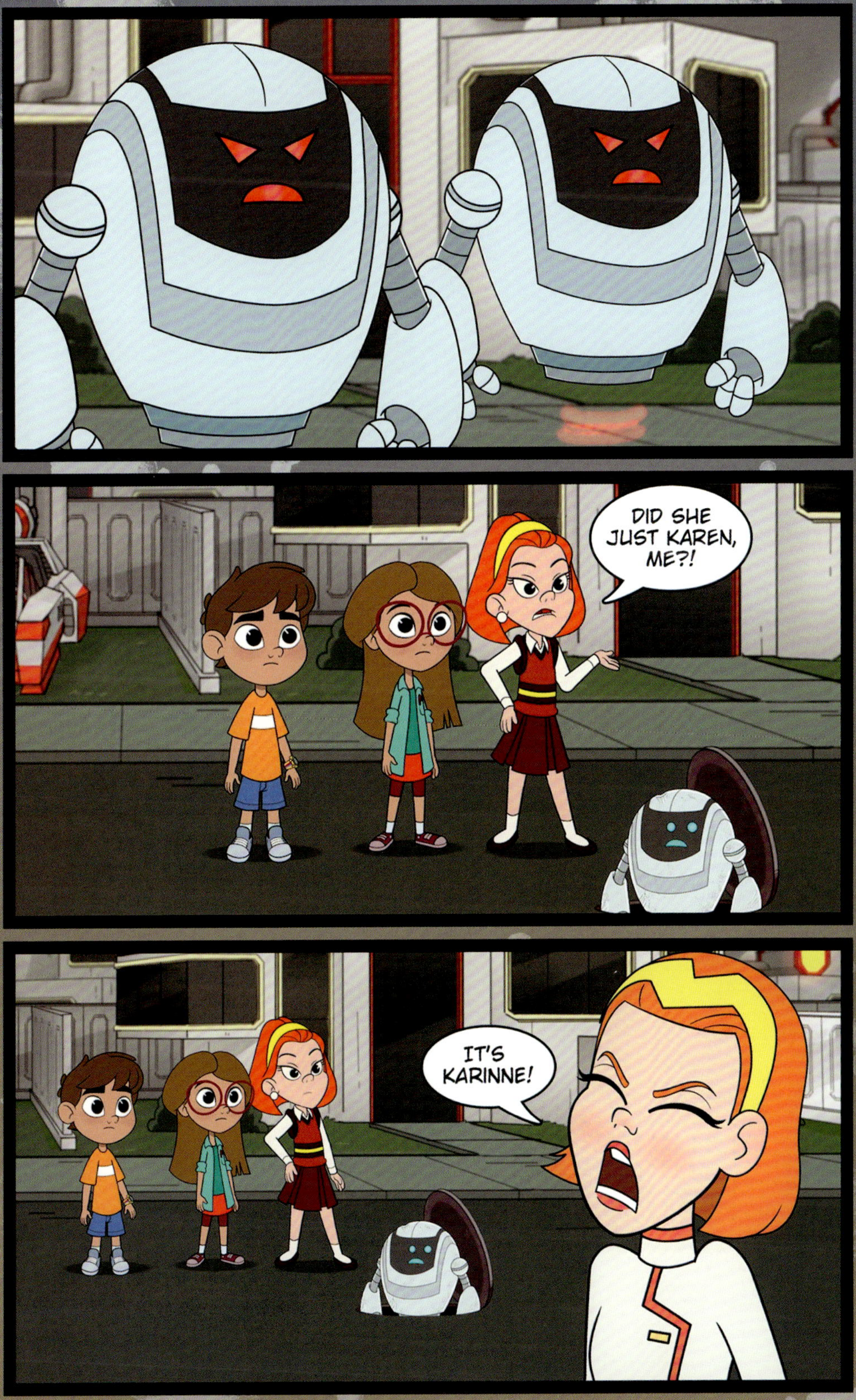
DID SHE JUST KAREN, ME?!
IT'S KARINNE!

LOOK! JAYWALKERS!

SPIN

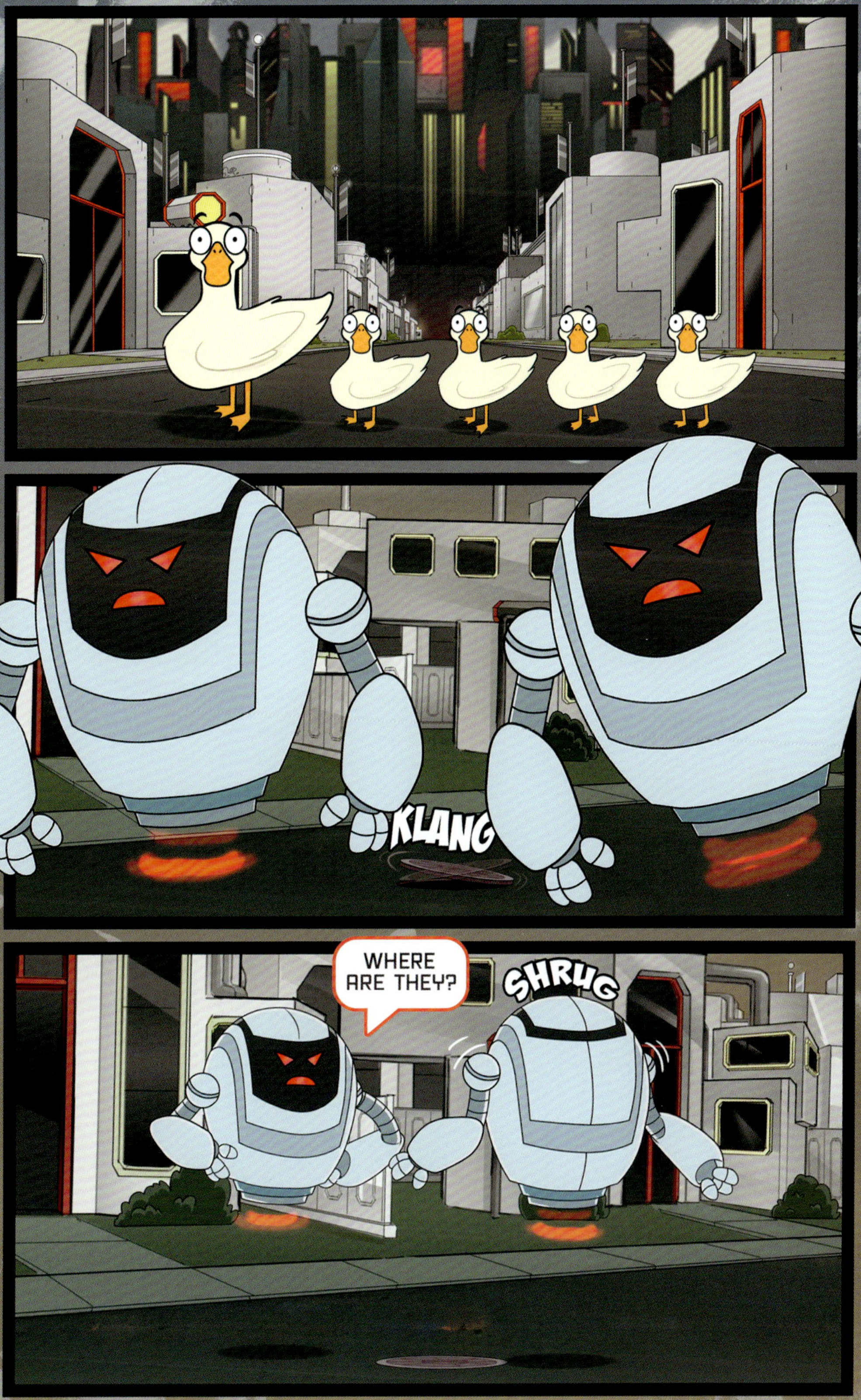
KLANG
WHERE ARE THEY?
SHRUG

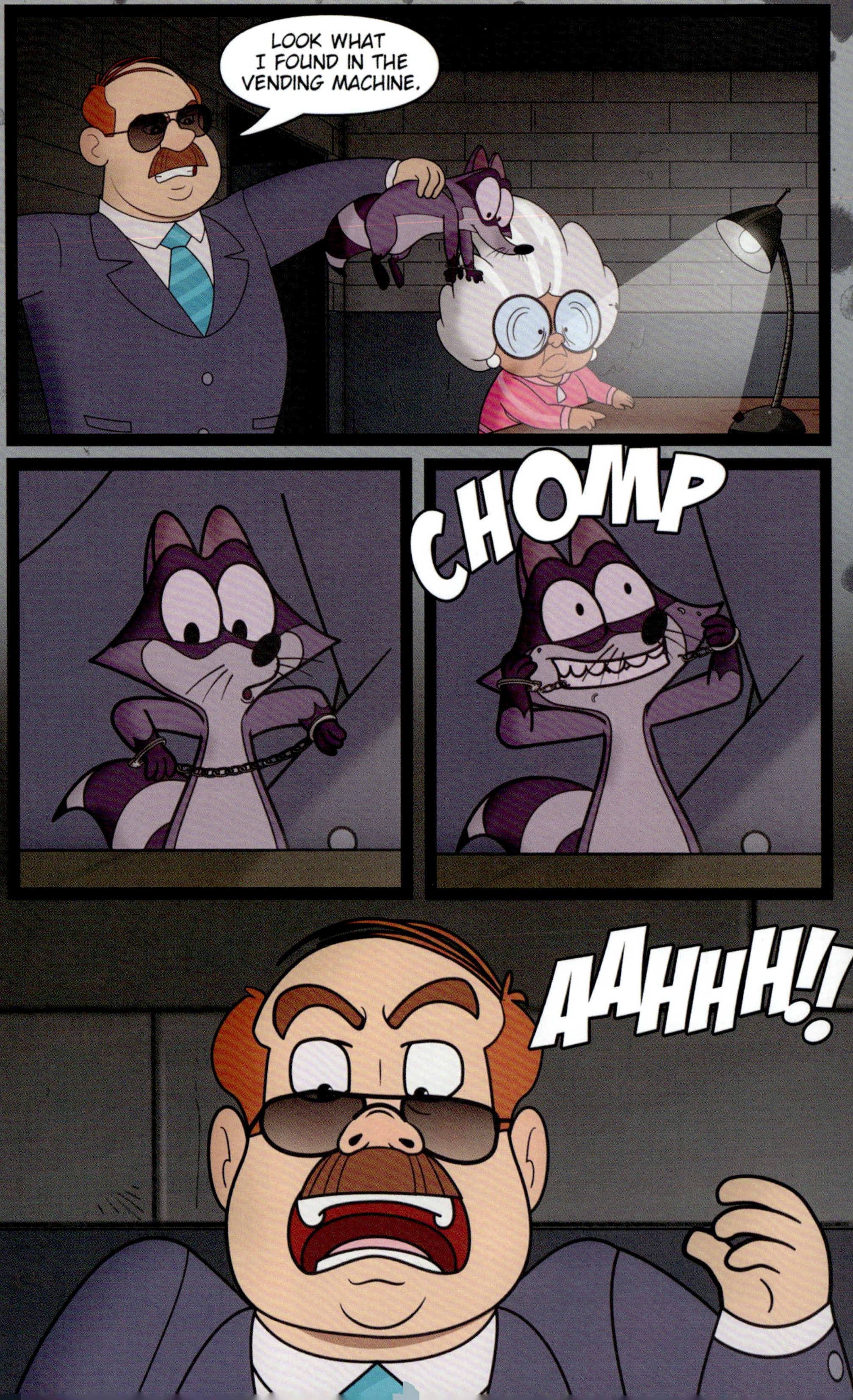
LOOK WHAT I FOUND IN THE VENDING MACHINE.
CHOMP
AAHHH!!

CLICK-CLICK
DON'T. DON'T YOU D-
NO DON'T, DON'T! DON'T!
GAH!
CRUNCH
CLICK-CLICK
CHOMP!

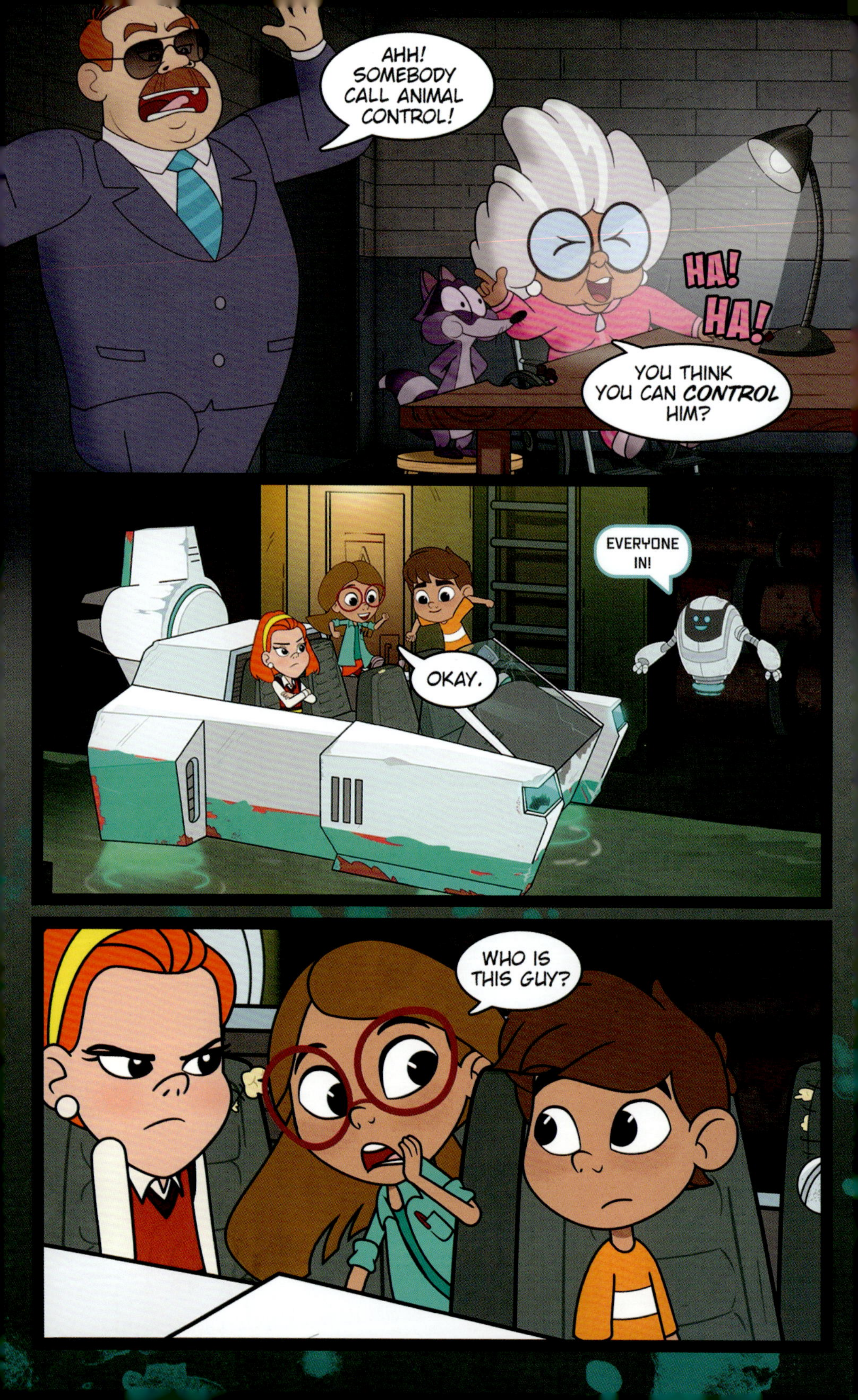
AHH! SOMEBODY CALL ANIMAL CONTROL!
HA! HA!
YOU THINK YOU CAN CONTROL HIM?
EVERYONE IN!
OKAY.
WHO IS THIS GUY?

I'M A REPROGRAMMED DROID, ORIGINALLY BUILT AS A TOUR GUIDE,

BUT NOW MY PURPOSE IS TO EDUCATE ANYONE INTERESTED IN THE REBELLION AGAINST TOTALITARIANISM.

BUT YOU CAN JUST CALL ME *STEVE*.

HI STEVE!

SHALL I EXTERMINATE THE ONE MEMBER OF YOUR PARTY WHO IS NOT INTERESTED?

ZZZRRR

NO, NO, HAHA, THAT'S OKAY!
HOW DID YOU KNOW ONE OF US WASN'T INTERESTED?
YOU SMILED WHEN I SAID "TOTALITARIANISM."

WHAT'S WRONG WITH THIS PLACE? BESIDES THOSE CUTE LITTLE DICTATOR ROBOTS.
HB MEGA-STORE

GROCERIES
YEAH! EVERYTHING DOES SEEM GREAT. YOU'VE GOT A BIG GROCERY STORE, A BIG POWER FACILITY...
AND THEY ALL HAVE THE SAME AMAZING PORTRAIT OF A MASKED FIGURE RULING OVER THEM!
:EYE-ROLL-EMOJI: THAT IS OUR BENEVOLENT LEADER. THE ONE RESPONSIBLE FOR OUR ONE-NOTE LIVES.
:EMOJI-WITH-THE-STRAIGHT-LINE-FOR-A-MOUTH:
WAIT, ARE YOU SPEAKING IN EMOJIS? FORGIVE US, WE'RE FROM A THOUSAND YEARS AGO.

AFTER YOUR GENERATION INVENTED EMOJIS, PEOPLE BECAME SO RELIANT ON THEM THEY BECAME PART OF THE ENGLISH LANGUAGE.

:LAUGHING-WHILE MOSTLY-CRYING EMOJI:

HONESTLY, FOR BEING A THOUSAND YEARS AHEAD OF US, YOU'D THINK BY NOW YOU'D LIVE IN SELF-FARMING HOUSEHOLDS AND TRAVEL BY TELEPORTATION!

YES, THAT SHOULD HAVE HAPPENED. :DISAPPOINTED-EMOJI:

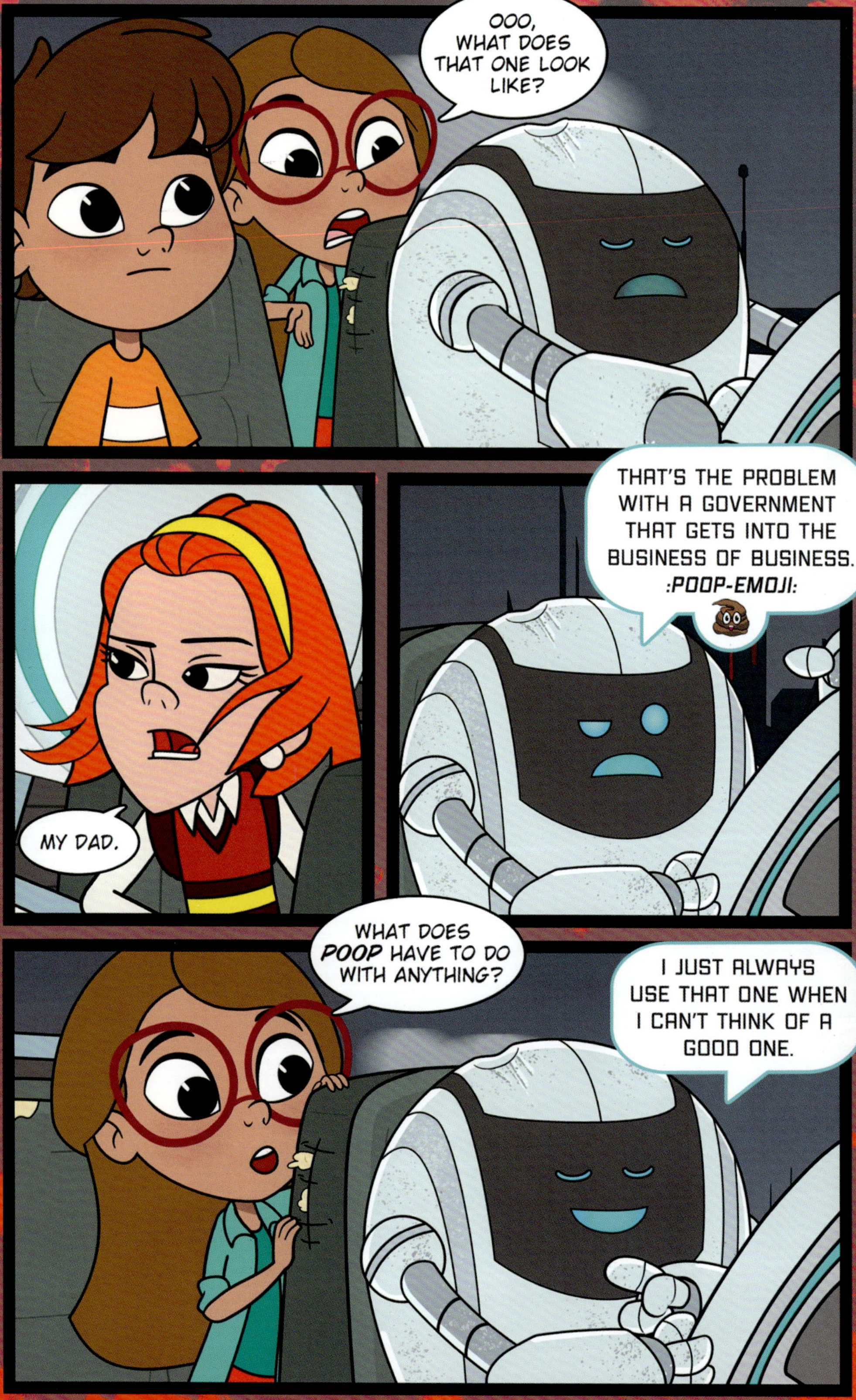
OOO, WHAT DOES THAT ONE LOOK LIKE?
MY DAD.
THAT'S THE PROBLEM WITH A GOVERNMENT THAT GETS INTO THE BUSINESS OF BUSINESS. :POOP-EMOJI:
WHAT DOES *POOP* HAVE TO DO WITH ANYTHING?
I JUST ALWAYS USE THAT ONE WHEN I CAN'T THINK OF A GOOD ONE.

SPEAKING OF WHICH, WE'RE APPROACHING THE DMV: THE DEPARTMENT OF MOTOR VEHICLES.

UGH, ONE TIME WE HAD TO GO WITH OUR MOM TO THE DMV TO RENEW HER DRIVER'S LICENSE, IT TOOK LIKE FIVE HOURS.

HASN'T CHANGED.

IF THE DMV WERE A PRIVATE BUSINESS, LIKE A PIZZA RESTAURANT...
PIZZA
THEY WOULD GET SO MANY COMPLAINTS ABOUT THE WAIT THAT THEY'D EITHER FIGURE OUT HOW TO MAKE IT FASTER, OR LOSE THEIR BUSINESS TO A BETTER PIZZA PLACE.

UH, EXCUSE ME, HOW LONG HAVE YOU BEEN HERE?
UGH, SINCE LAST NIGHT.
PARKING VIOLATION
P
$3,000,000,000
I HAD TO TAKE THE DAY OFF OF WORK, AND I STILL DON'T KNOW HOW I'M GOING TO PAY THIS THREE BILLION DOLLAR PARKING TICKET.

THREE BILLION DOLLARS?

WHAT, YOU THOUGHT THAT INFLATION WOULD... STOP?

RRAAWWWWWRR!

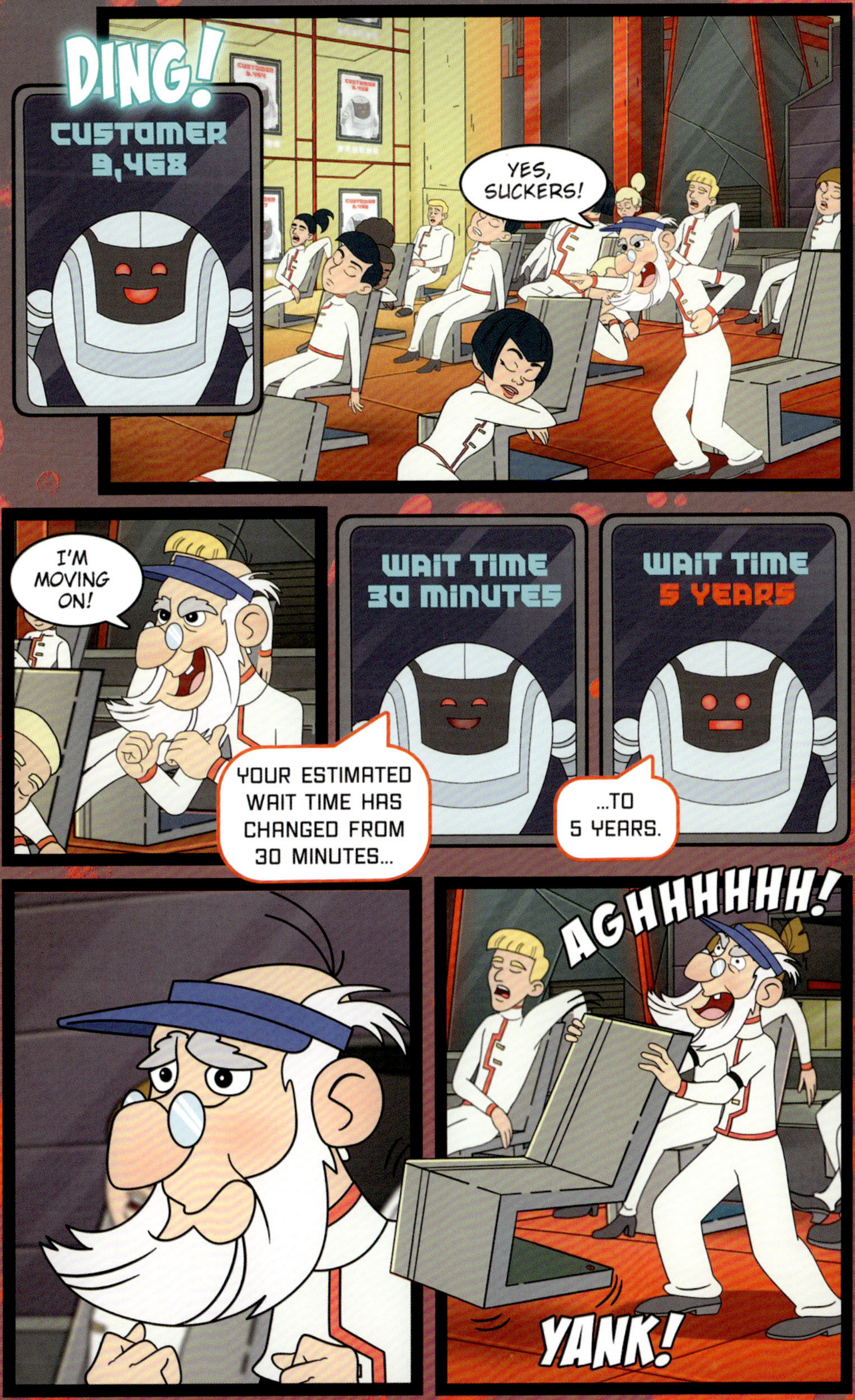
DING!
CUSTOMER 9,468
YES, SUCKERS!
I'M MOVING ON!
WAIT TIME 30 MINUTES
WAIT TIME 5 YEARS
YOUR ESTIMATED WAIT TIME HAS CHANGED FROM 30 MINUTES...
...TO 5 YEARS.
AGHHHHHH!
YANK!

THE GOVERNMENT RUNS THE DMV AND DOESN'T ALLOW PRIVATE COMPANIES TO COMPETE WITH THEM.

SO YOU'RE FORCED TO EITHER USE THEM OR NOT DRIVE AT ALL.

WOOOOSH

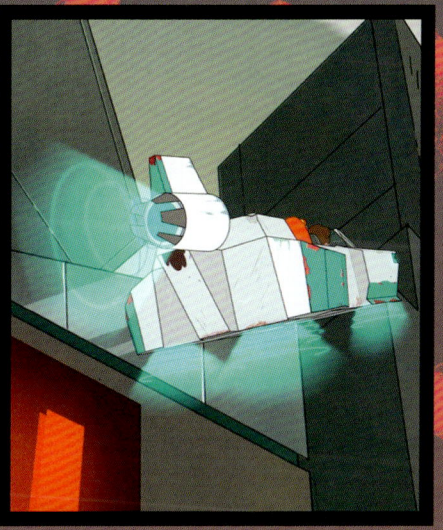

"I HAD NO CLUE COMPETITION COULD APPLY TO GOVERNMENT BUSINESSES TOO!"

"WHEN WE MADE OUR CORN DOG STAND, WE LEARNED HOW COMPETITION MAKES BUSINESSES BETTER."

"KARINNE HERE IS TO THANK FOR THAT."

"DON'T BRING ME INTO THIS! I LIKE THE DMV, IT'S... ORDERLY."

TODAY ALMOST EVERY BUSINESS IS RUN EXCLUSIVELY BY THE GOVERNMENT AND EVERY CUSTOMER SUFFERS, EVEN IF THEY DON'T KNOW IT.

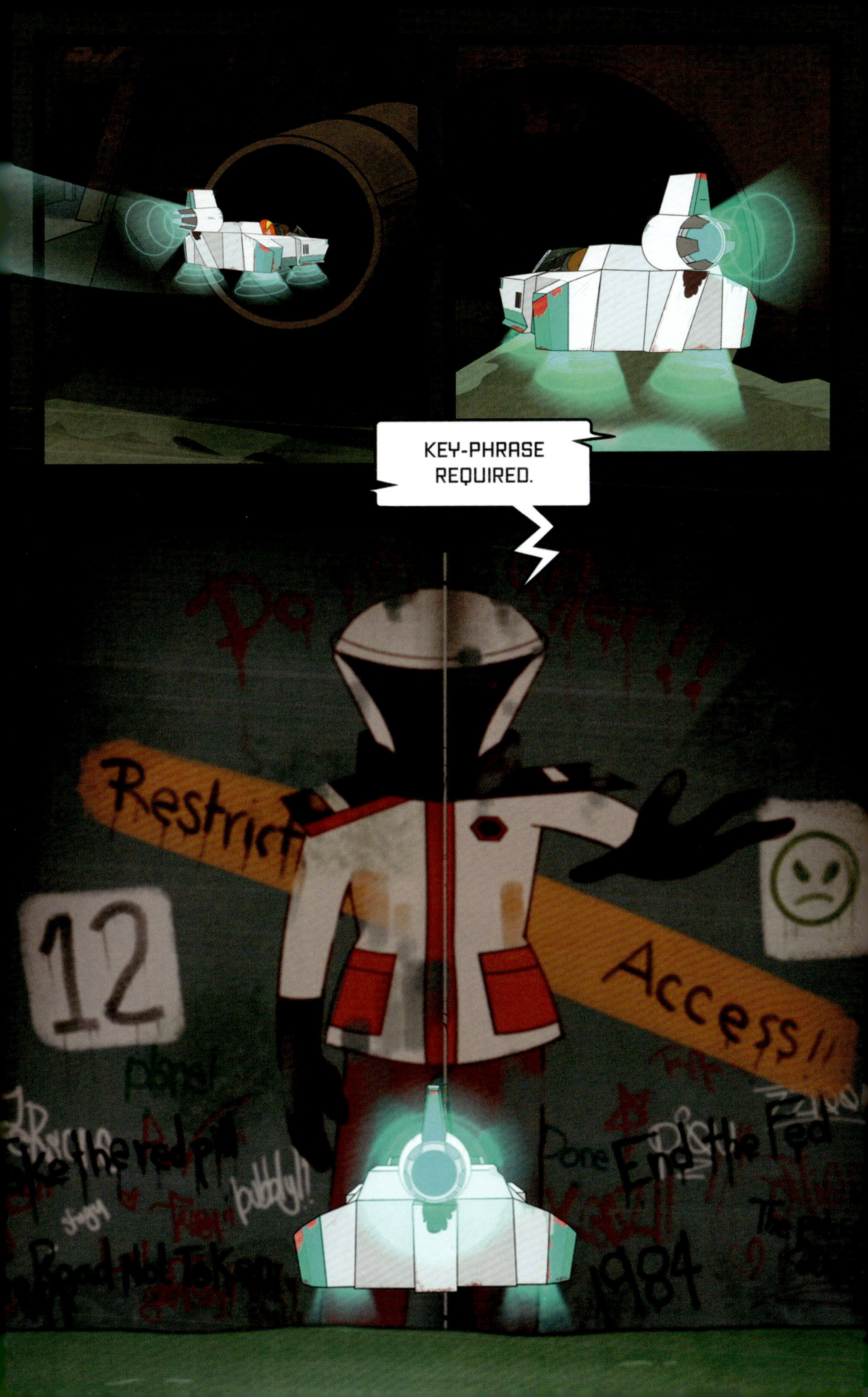
KEY-PHRASE REQUIRED.
Restrict
Access!!
12
End the Fed
1984

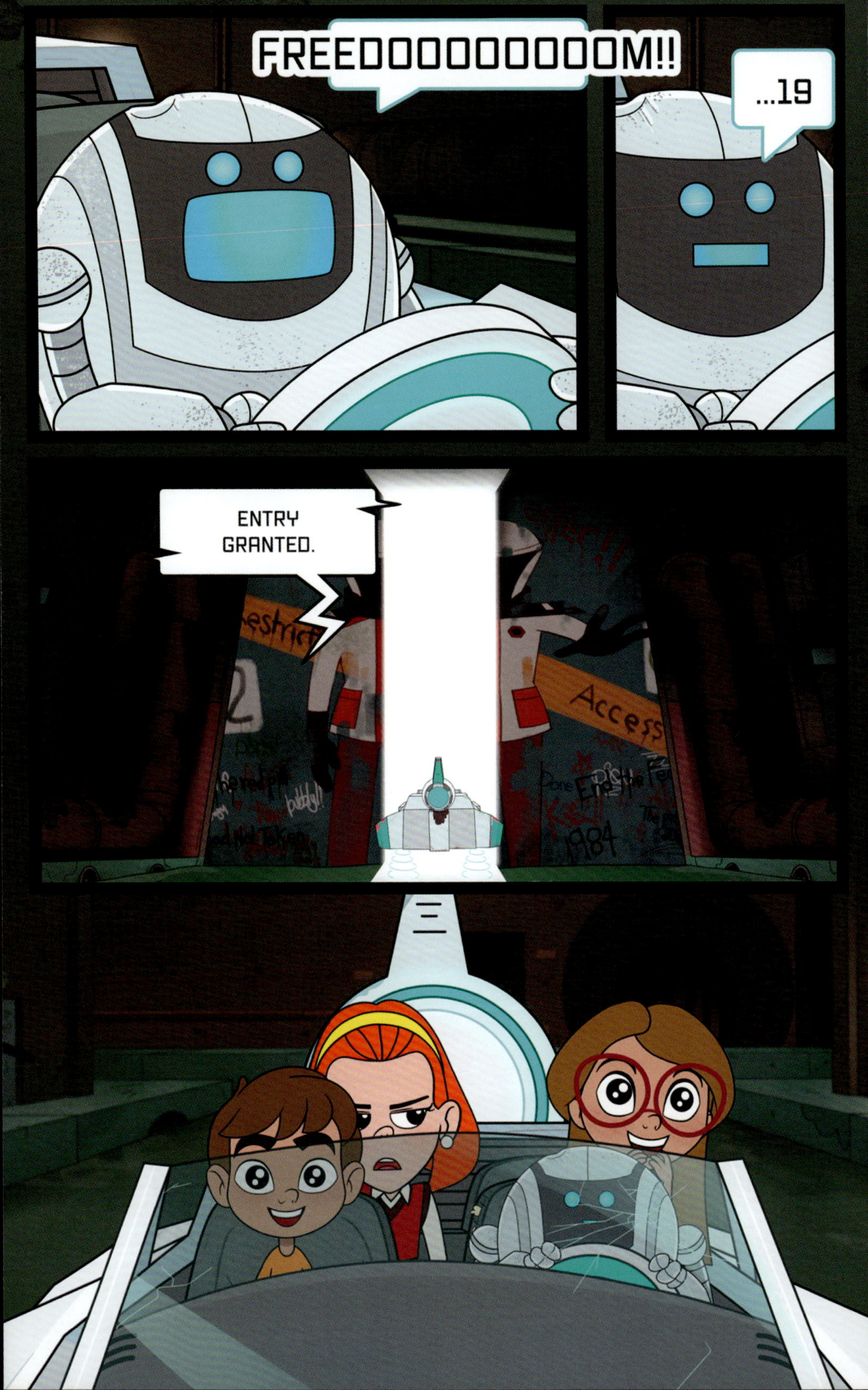
FREEDOOOOOOOOOM!!
...19
ENTRY GRANTED.

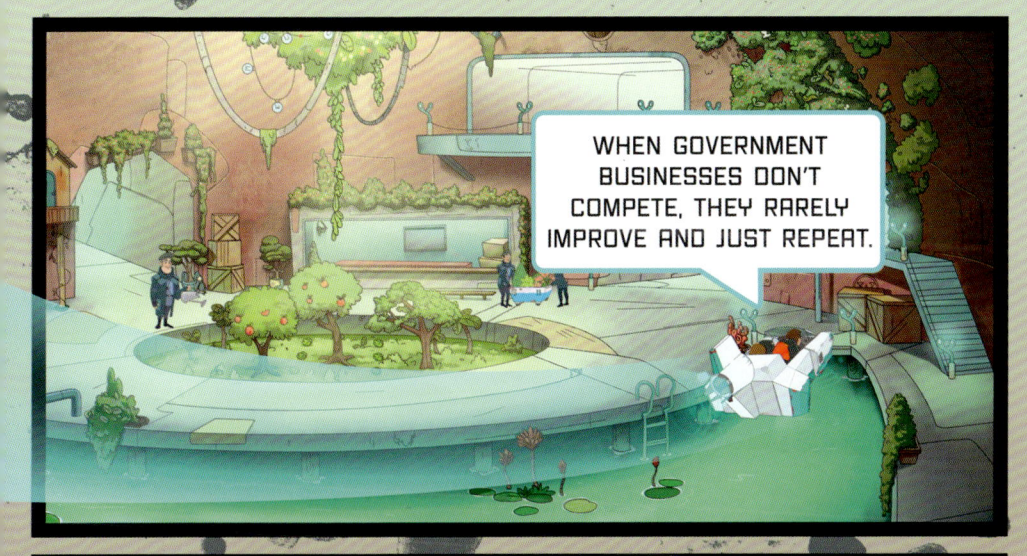

WHEN GOVERNMENT BUSINESSES DON'T COMPETE, THEY RARELY IMPROVE AND JUST REPEAT.

"SO, HOW DO WE FIX IT?"

"LET OTHER PRIVATE BUSINESSES COMPETE."

"AND LET THE PEOPLE CHOOSE!"

"UGH!"

"YOU MEAN, LIKE CHOOSING WHICH GOVERNMENT SERVICES TO USE?"

"PRECISELY."

"THAT DOESN'T WORK! PEOPLE ONLY NEED ONE CHOICE. ONE SAFE, **GOVERNMENT APPROVED** CHOICE! LET THE GOVERNMENT CONTROL MEDICAL CARE, RETIREMENT FUNDS... *THE CHILDREN!*"

"I MEAN... *SCHOOLS.*"

BEFORE 1844, THE ONLY WAY TO SEND MAIL IN THE US WAS THROUGH THE GOVERNMENT-RUN POSTAL SERVICE.

SENDING MAIL BECAME SUPER SLOW AND EXPENSIVE.

BUT THEN, BECAUSE OF PRIVATE MAIL COMPETITORS, LIKE UPS AND FEDEX, THE GOVERNMENT WAS FORCED TO IMPROVE. SENDING MAIL BECAME CHEAPER AND FASTER FOR EVERYONE.

NOW INSTEAD OF WAITING WEEKS FOR A PACKAGE, IT ARRIVES IN DAYS.

WOW.
IMAGINE HOW MUCH BETTER THE DMV WOULD BE IF MULTIPLE PRIVATE COMPANIES COMPETED TO GIVE YOU A DRIVER'S LICENSE.
I WON'T BELIEVE IT! YOU'RE JUST JEALOUS OF THE GOVERNMENT UTOPIA RIGHT OUTSIDE THOSE DOORS!
CONTROL WORKS! IT ***ALWAYS WORKS!*** YOU'RE JUST TRYING TO SCARE US.

KARINNE! WAIT!
GASP
YOU WERE SEEN FLYING IN AN UNAUTHORIZED VEHICLE. YOU ARE UNDER ARREST.

:FACE-WITH STEAM-FROM NOSE-EMOJI:

GOTCHA REBEL.

:THAT-ONE FINGER-EMOJI:

OFFENSE TAKEN!

GASP *GASP*

QUICK, ETHAN! ACTIVATE THE WHEELCHAIR!

GLUB GLUB GLUB

IT'S EMPTY!

AHHHHHH!

STILL NO SIGN OF YOUR WHEELCHAIR OF MASS DESTRUCTION...

BUT WE'LL WAIT.

GOVERNMENT WAITING TO GET WORK DONE? IT CAN'T BE TRUE!

WHAT IS *IN* THIS THING?!

SHAKE SHAKE

KLANK

KLONK KLANK GROWL GAH! HISSSSSS

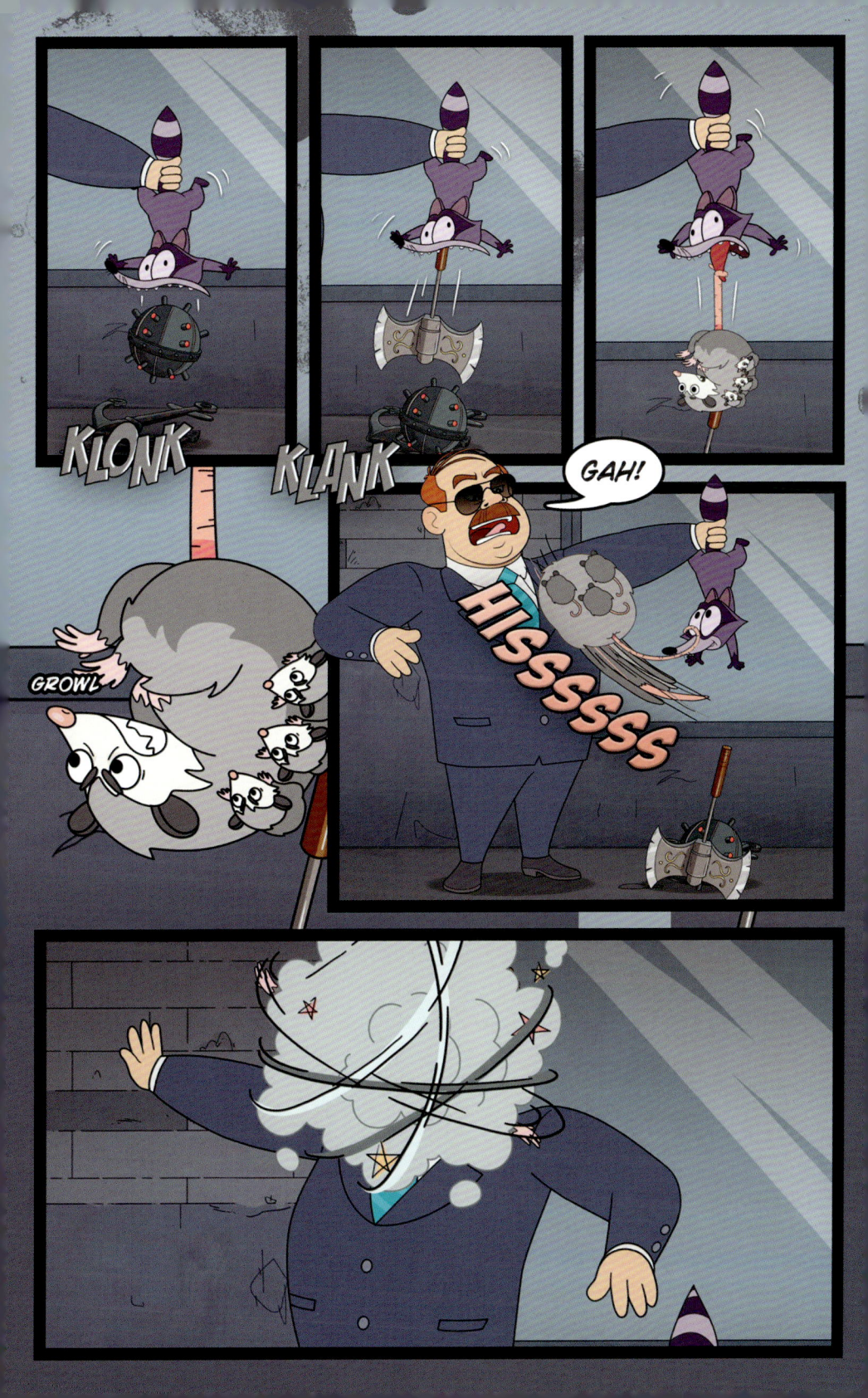

I WANT MY PHONE CALL.
WE'RE NOT DONE HERE.
SLAM!
OOF!
I. WANT. MY. PHONE CALL.

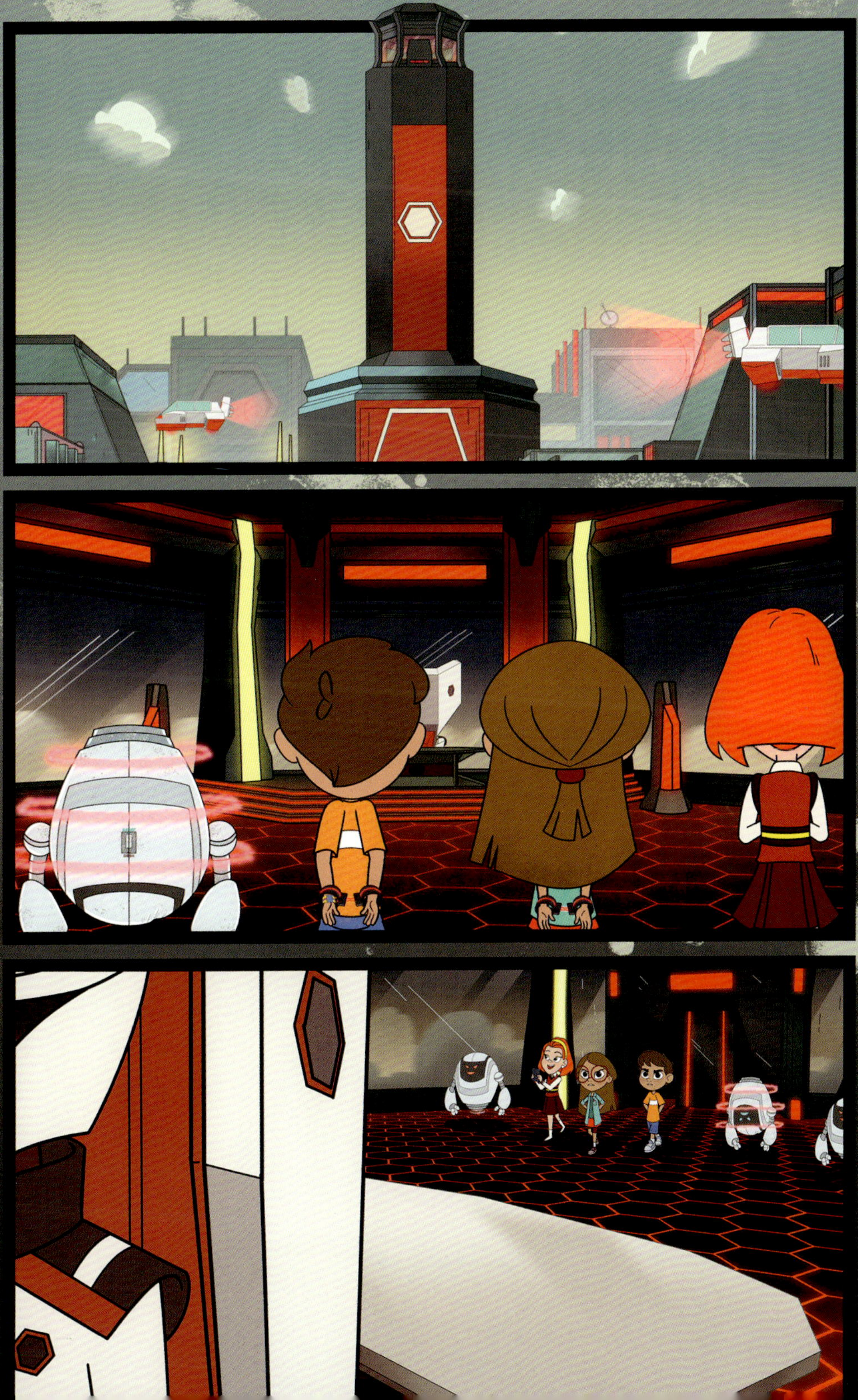

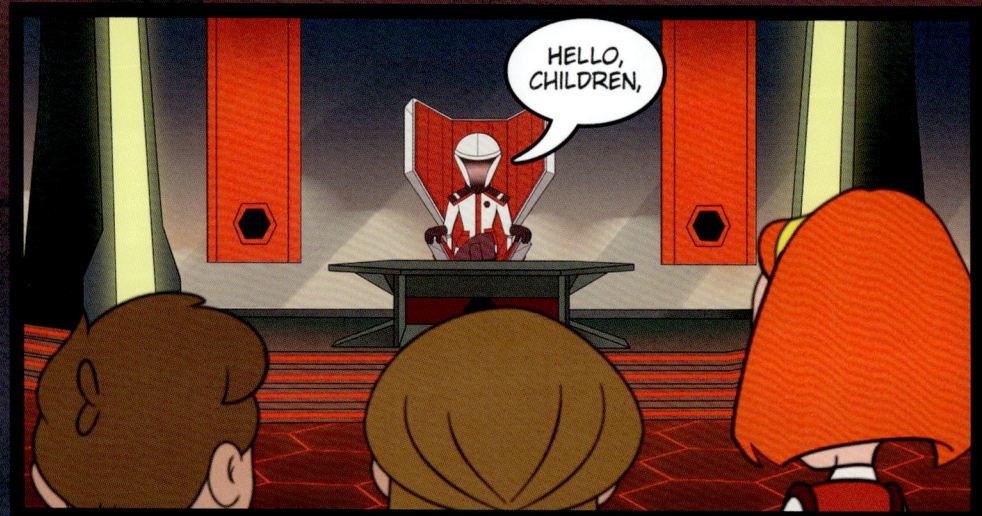

SNAP

CLICK

OKAY, I PROMISE THIS IS NOT FOR BLACKMAIL.

IT'S FOR MY VISION BOARD.

HELLO, CHILDREN,

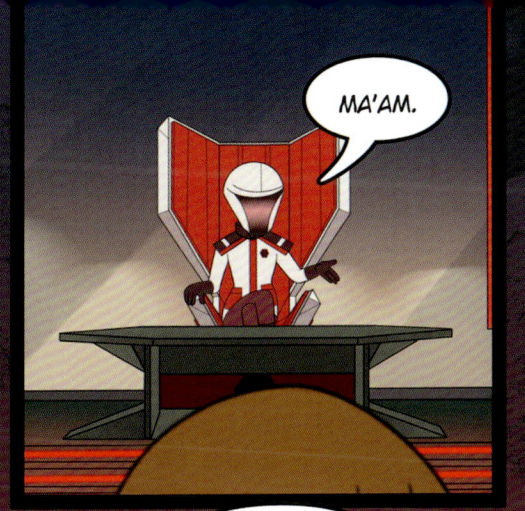

MA'AM.

WELCOME...
...TO YOUR JUDGMENT DAY!

HAHAHA HAHA

OOOO! "WELCOME TO MY JUDGMENT DAY."

SNAP!
GREAT, SOMEONE FLIPPED THIS ONE TO 'REBELLION MODE'.
REBEL
OBEY
NO, NO NO! YOU CA-
CLICK!
REBEL
OBEY

STEVE!

MY ROBO-HELPERS DETECTED SOMETHING INTERESTING ABOUT YOU KIDS.

YOU'RE HERE ILLEGALLY... FROM THE PAST.

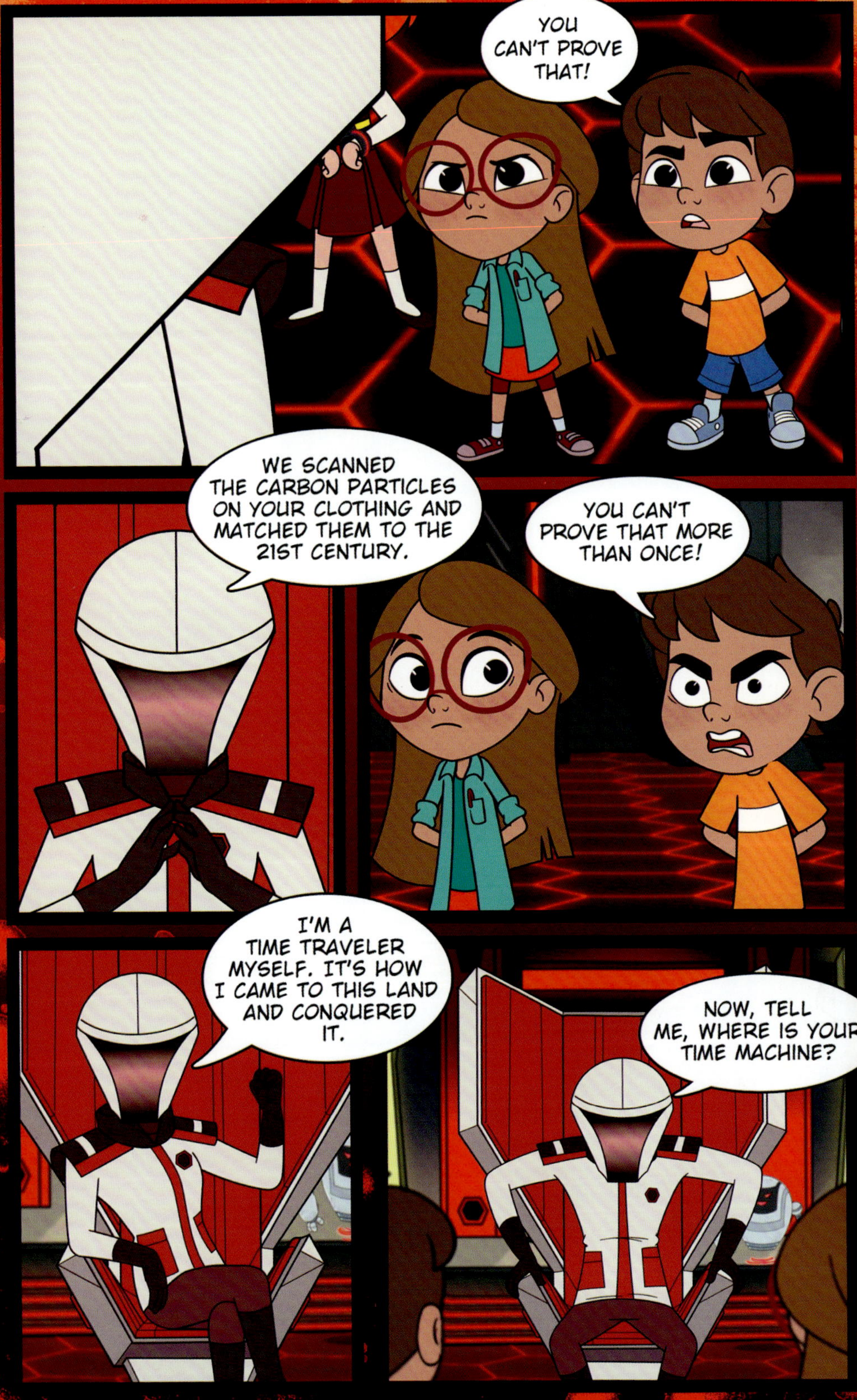
YOU CAN'T PROVE THAT!
WE SCANNED THE CARBON PARTICLES ON YOUR CLOTHING AND MATCHED THEM TO THE 21ST CENTURY.
YOU CAN'T PROVE THAT MORE THAN ONCE!
I'M A TIME TRAVELER MYSELF. IT'S HOW I CAME TO THIS LAND AND CONQUERED IT.
NOW, TELL ME, WHERE IS YOUR TIME MACHINE?

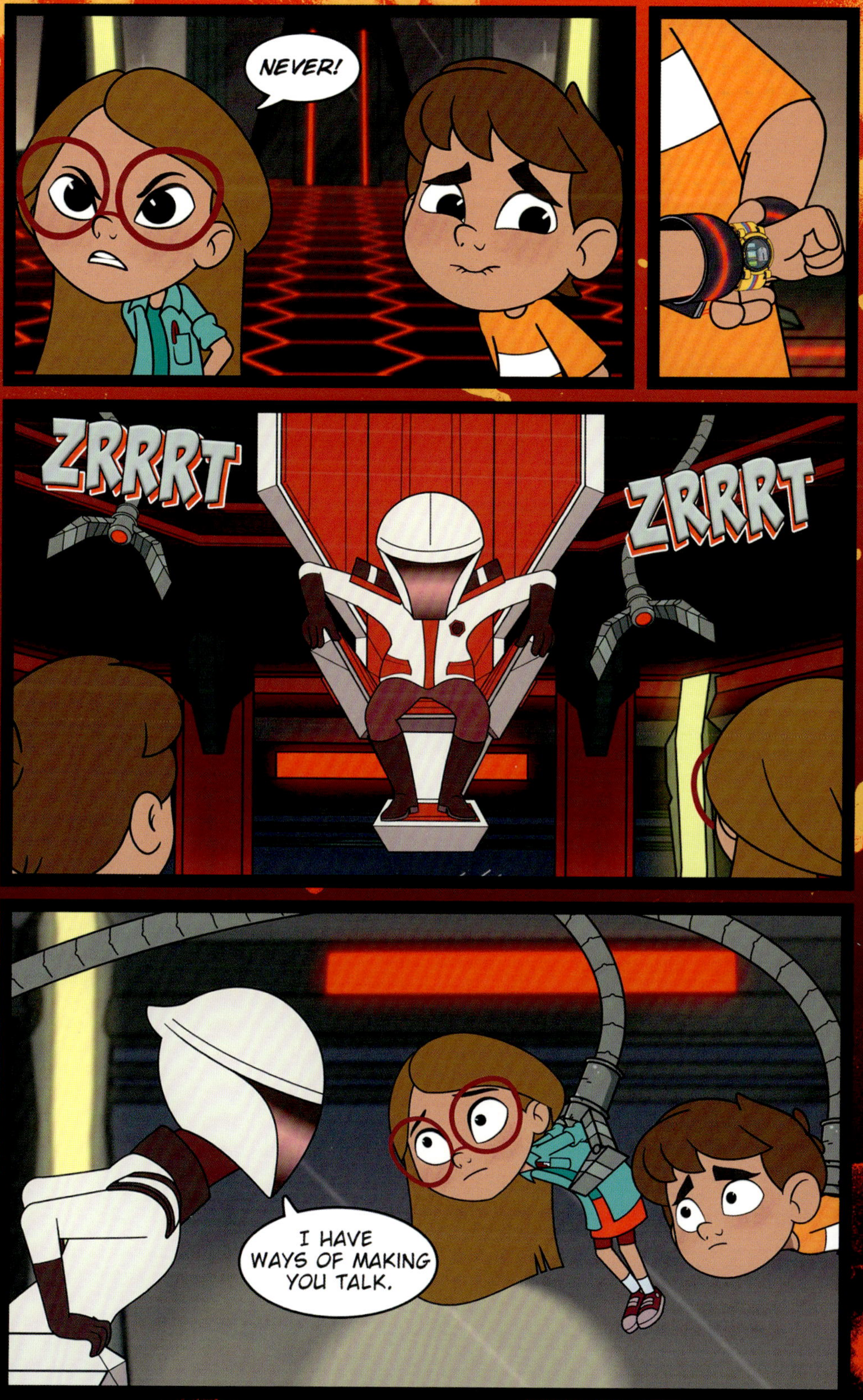
NEVER!
ZRRRT
ZRRRT
I HAVE WAYS OF MAKING YOU TALK.

WE CAN START BY MAKING YOU WAIT IN THE NON-PRIORITY LINE OF THE DMV.

I DON'T DRIVE!

WELL YOU'LL BE OLD ENOUGH TO BY THE TIME YOU'RE THROUGH WITH THE DMV LINE.

WHO *ARE* YOU?

MY HERO!

AND WHY DO YOU HIDE YOUR FACE?

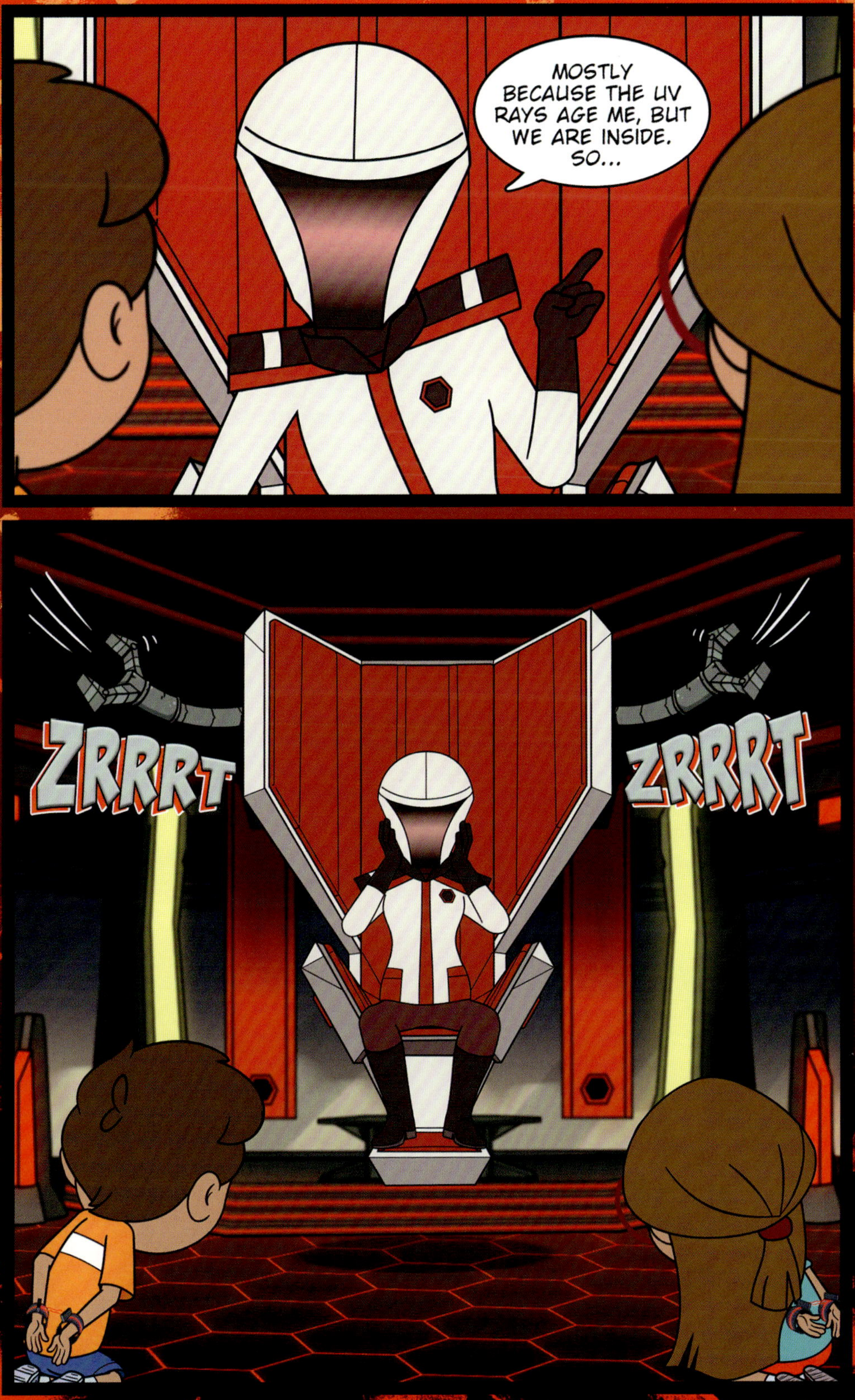
MOSTLY BECAUSE THE UV RAYS AGE ME, BUT WE ARE INSIDE. SO...
ZRRRT
ZRRRT

UHH... WAS THIS SUPPOSED TO BE SOME SORT OF BIG REVEAL?

POOF!

GRANDMA!??
HOW DARE YOU! I'M 25!
JUST FOR THAT YOU'LL WORK A MONTH AT THE DMV FOR NO PAY!
HOW DID YOU BECOME A TOTALITARIAN DICTATOR?

AS A GIRL, I GREW UP IN CUBA.

I SAW THE HORRORS OF INCOMPETENT COMMUNIST LEADERS FIRST HAND.

I THOUGHT "WHAT IF SOMEONE SMART AND CAPABLE COULD RUN THINGS INSTEAD?"

WITH MY BRILLIANCE AND TECHNOLOGY, WE COULD FINALLY GET RID OF HUNGER, CRIME, AND POVERTY.
AND SO I STUDIED.
MANIFOLDS
TENSORS
QUANTUM MECHANICS

I PREDICTED WHEN THE WORLD WOULD BE RIPE FOR A GOVERNMENT TAKEOVER.
I BUILT A TIME MACHINE.
EINSTEIN
THE COMMUNIST MANIFESTO
MEIN KAMPF
DAS KAPITAL
BRRZZT

AND I CONQUERED.

BUT, YOUR PLAN WON'T WORK, GRANDMA.

ZRRRT ZRRRT

STOP CALLING ME THAT!

HEY!
THAT'S MY TIME...
WATCH.
OH! SO
THIS IS THEIR TIME
MACHINE? GOOD
WORK.
TAKE THESE
KIDS TO THE
BRAINWASHER
3000.
NOOOO!

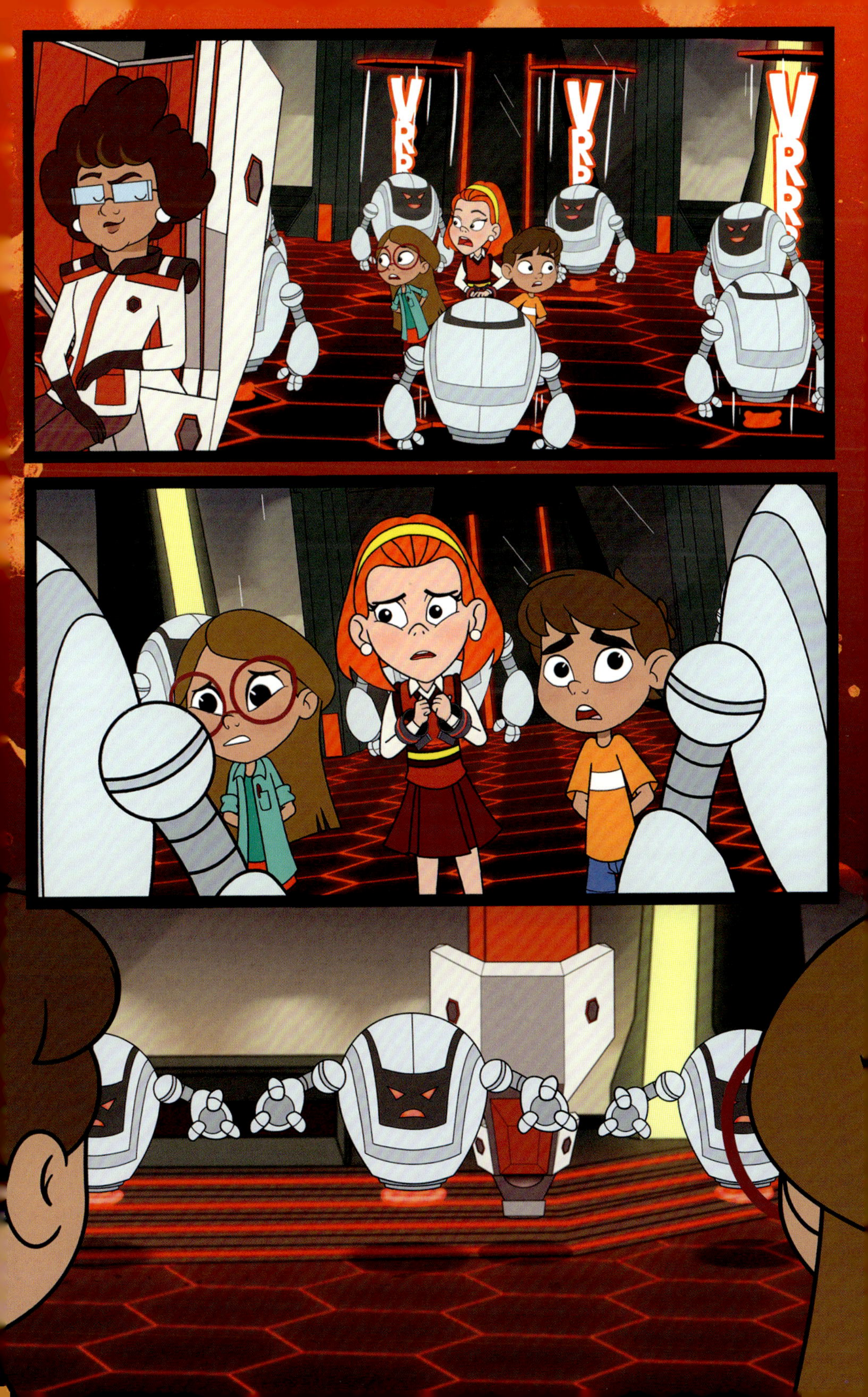
VRR
VR
VRR

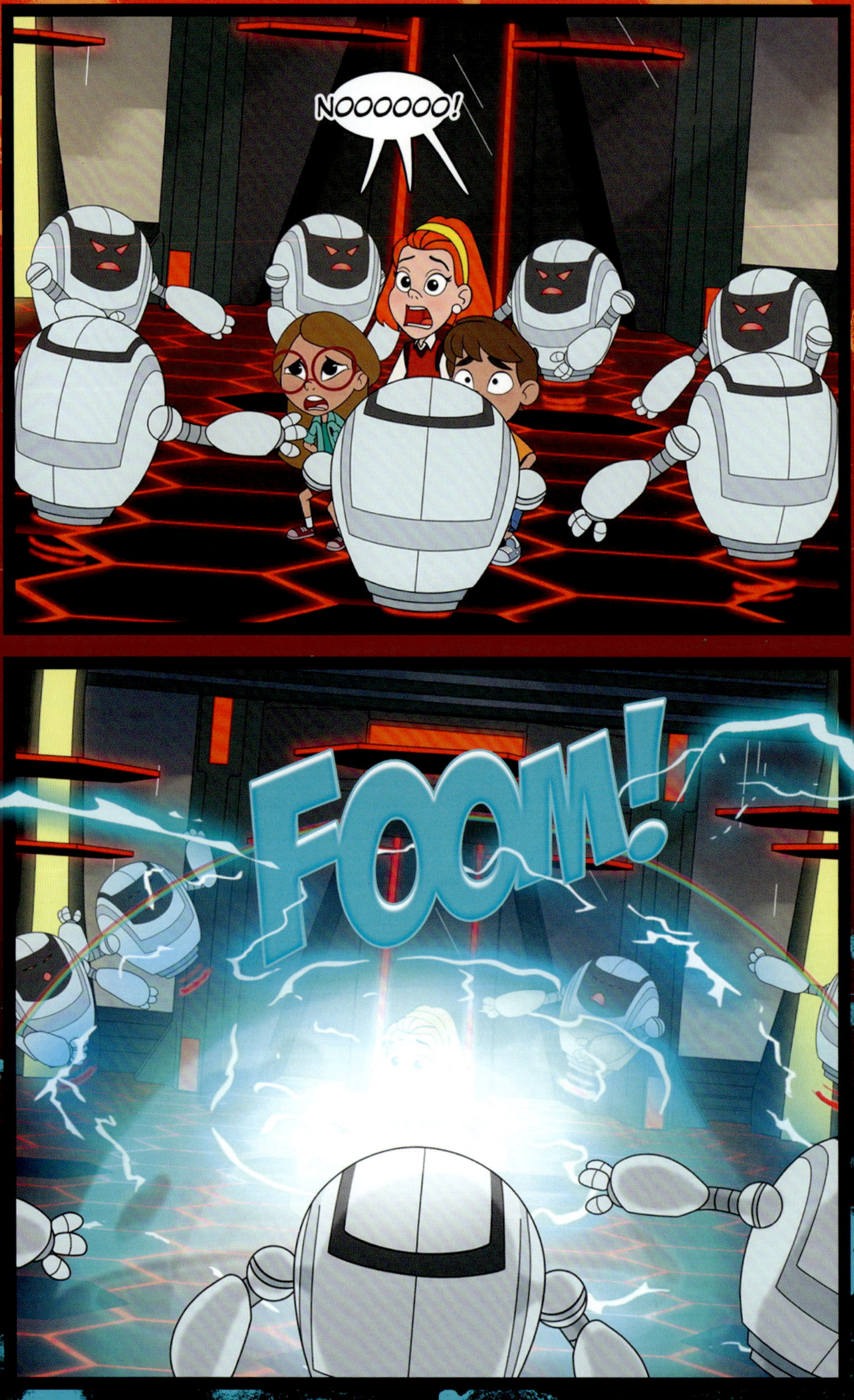
NOOOOOO!
FOOM!

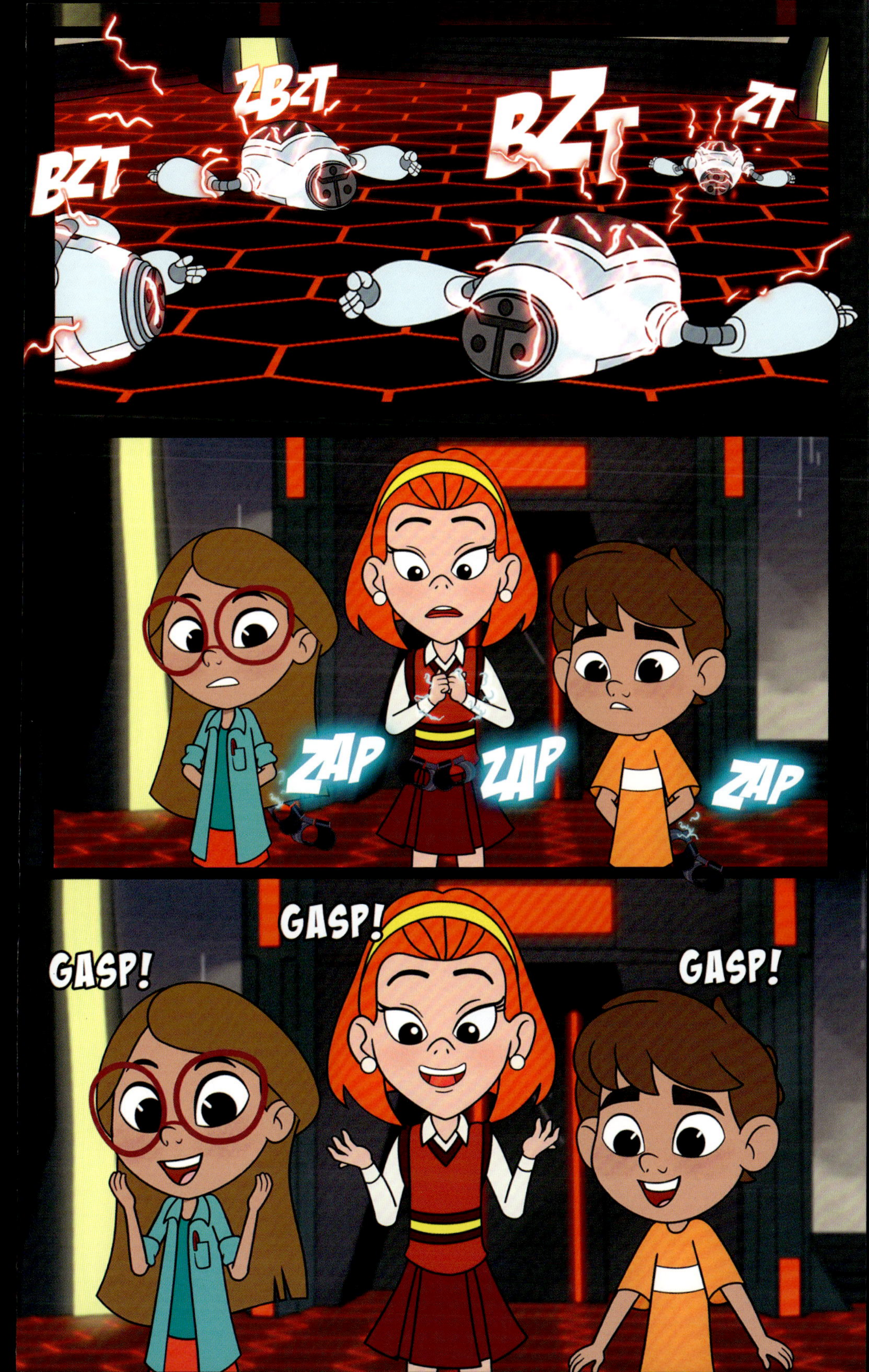
BZT
ZBZT
BZT
ZT
ZAP
ZAP
ZAP
GASP!
GASP!
GASP!

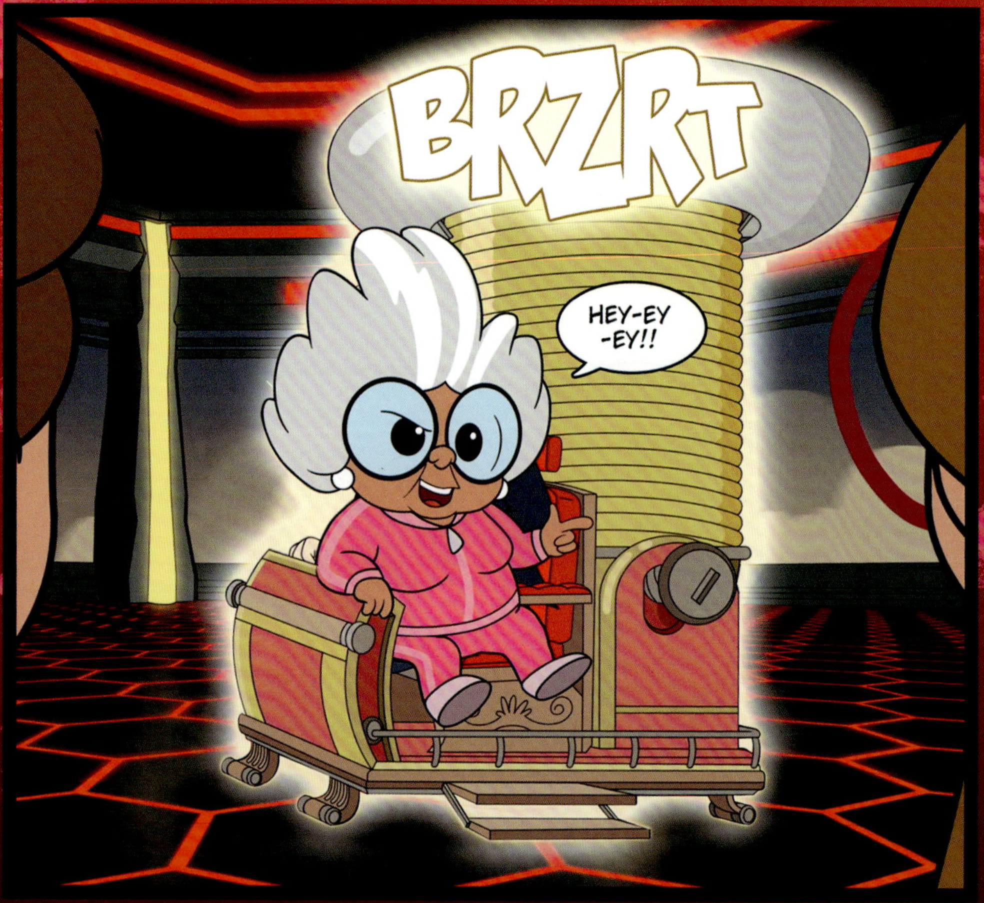
BRZRT
HEY-EY
-EY!!
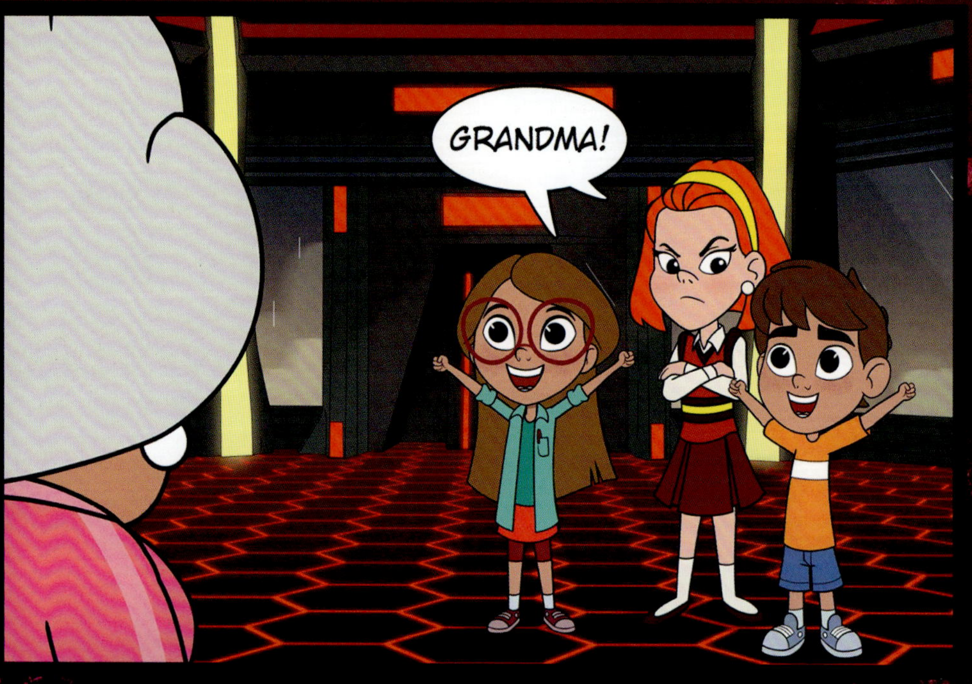
GRANDMA!

...AND NIKOLA TESLA WITH A TIME MACHINE?!
STEVE, FREEDOM 76!
FREEDOM 76

REBEL
OBEY
CLICK!
REBEL
OBEY
I'M FREE!
HOP ON, GRANDMA!
OH OKAY... YOU'RE OVER THE WEIGHT LIMIT.

GRACIAS TESSI!
OF COURSE, GABRIELA!
BRRZZT
HOW? I DON'T UNDERSTAND!
I GOT MY PHONE CALL.

WHO ARE YOU?
SOMEONE WHO REGRETS ALL OF THIS. NOW LEAVE THE NIÑOS ALONE!
WAKE UP, GABBY. FORCE DOESN'T WORK.
I'LL FORCE YOU...
...TO EAT THOSE WORDS!
ROBO-HELPERS!

DEREK, FREE FOOD!

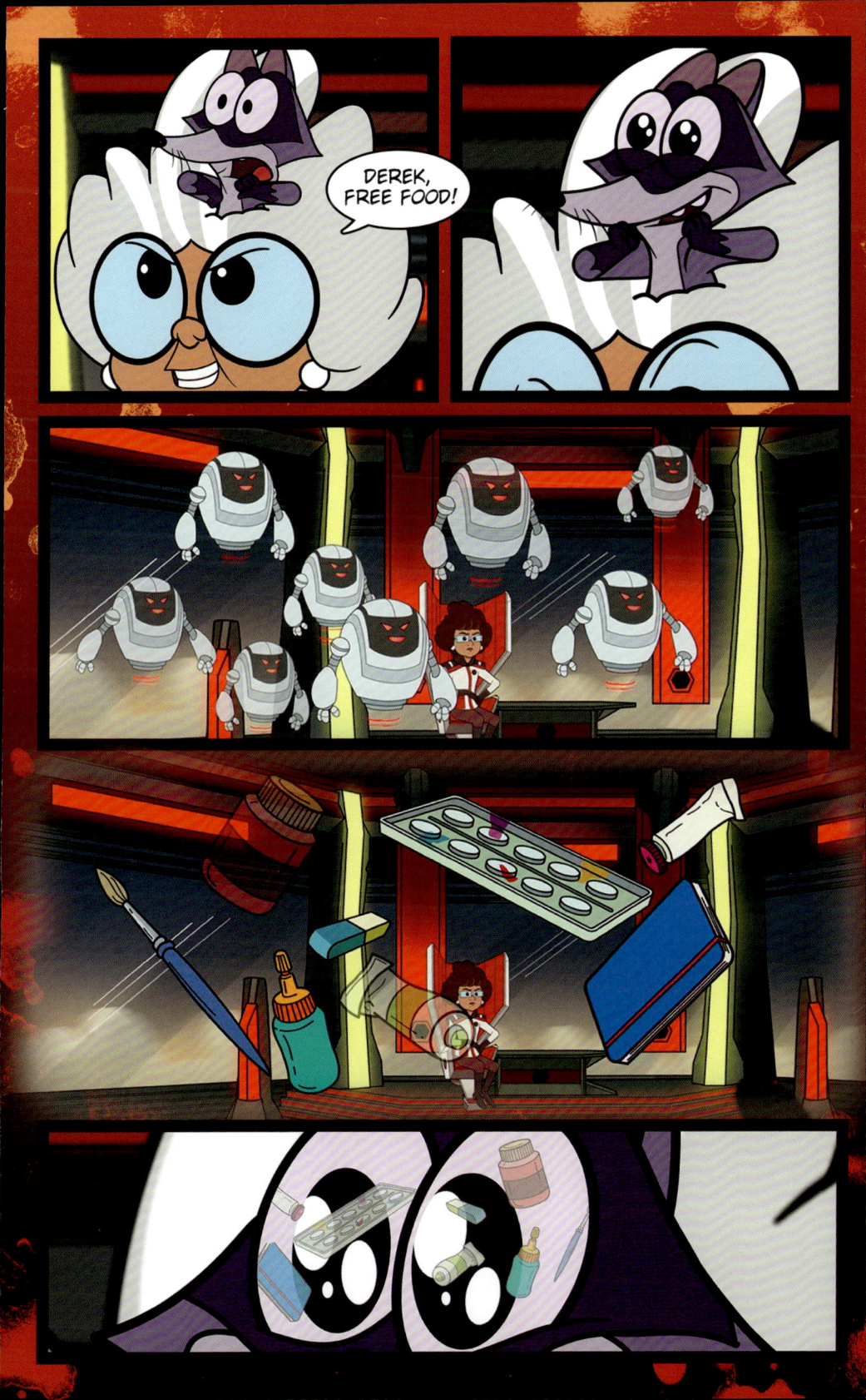

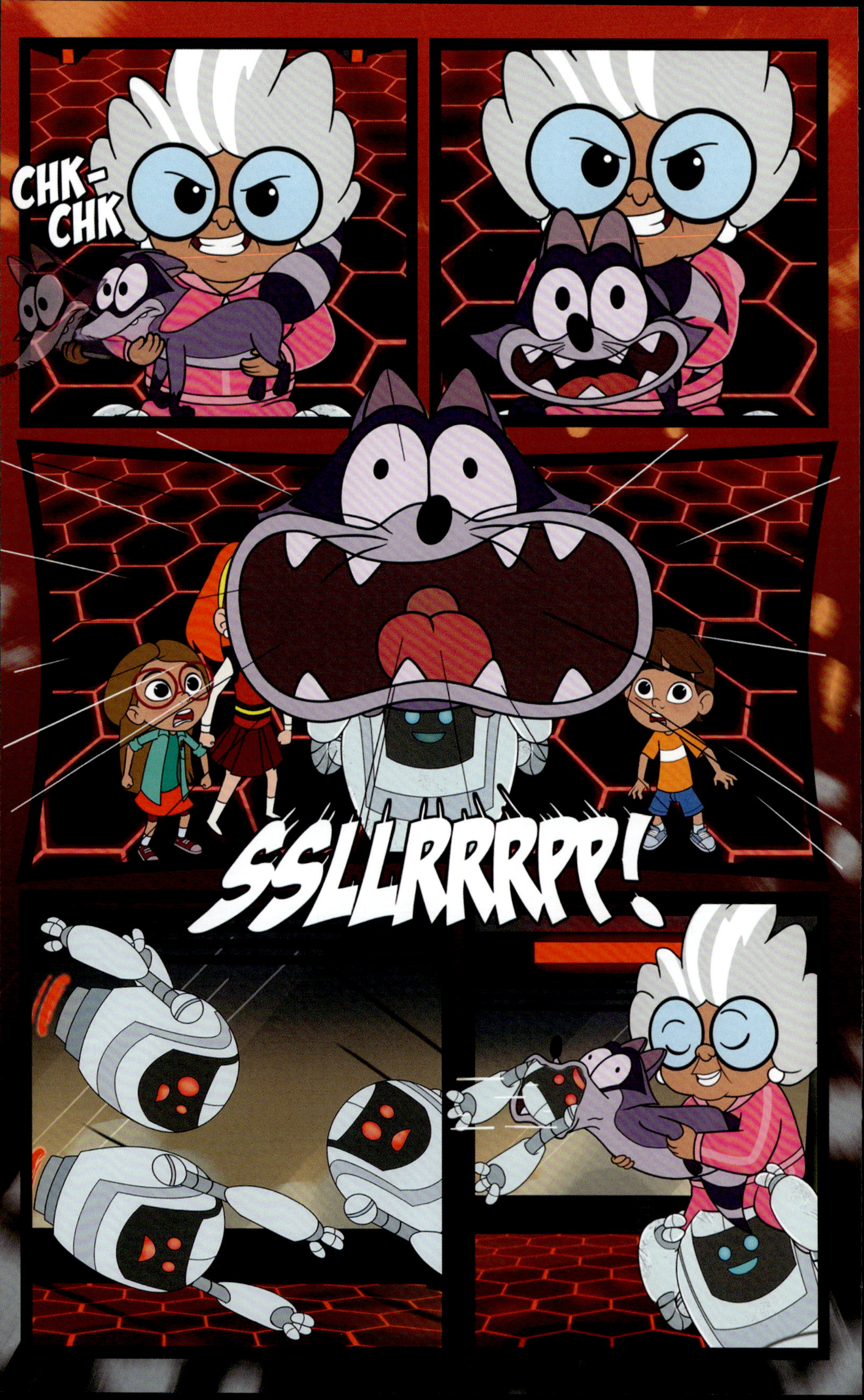
CHK-CHK
SSLLRRRPP!

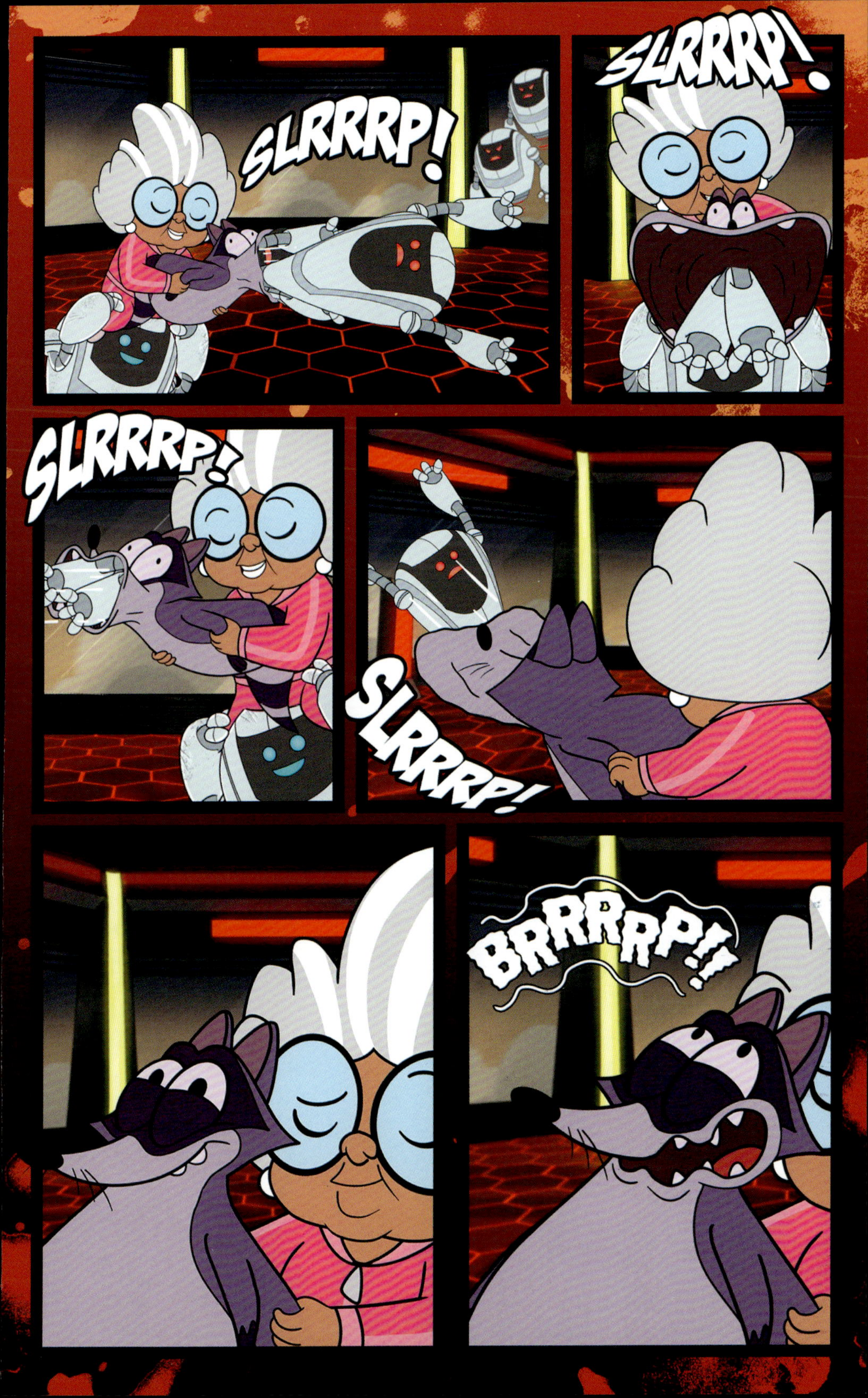
SLRRRP!
SLRRRP!
SLRRRP!
SLRRRP!
BRRRRRP!!

PEOPLE DON'T WANT FREEDOM, THEY WANT SAFETY.
FVSH
BUT YOU CAN'T SAVE THEM.
NOT THIS WAY.
FWIP
FWIP
NOT WITH FORCE AND LACK OF CHOICES.

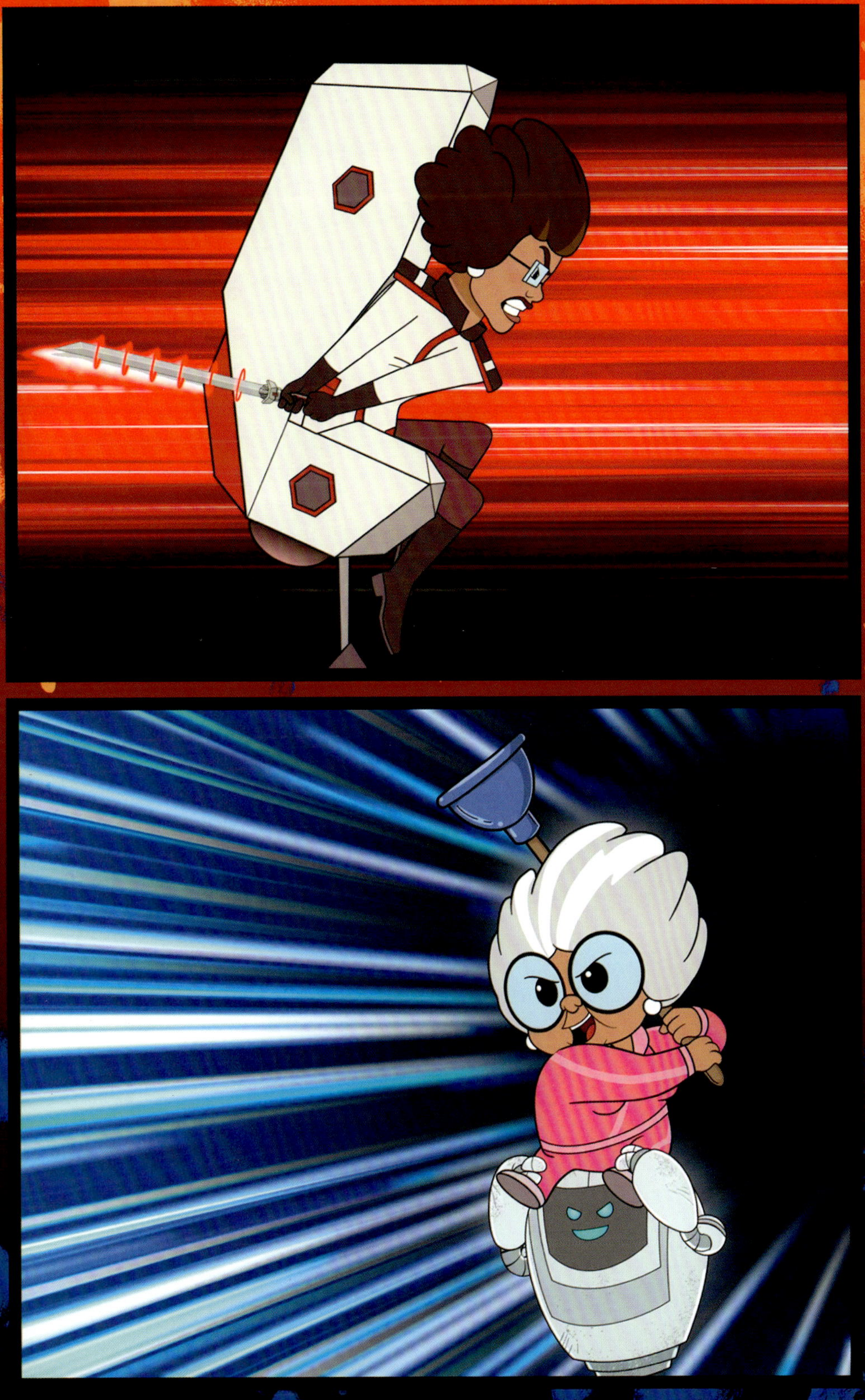

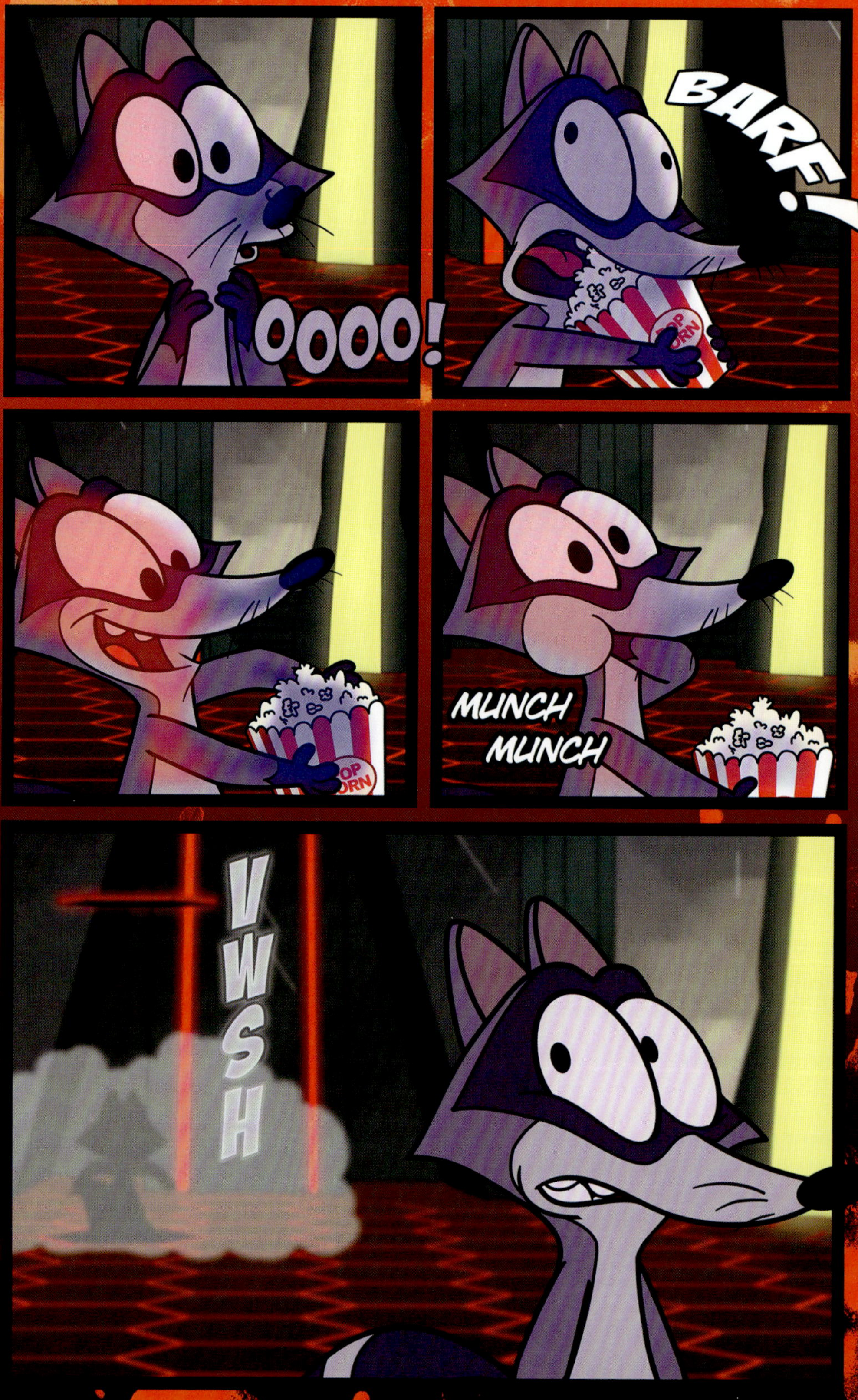
OOOO!
BARF!
POP CORN
POP CORN
MUNCH
MUNCH
VWSH

HRGAMAHRMABR!

HMMM?

FWIP

GRrrrr

I did not see that coming.

HORF

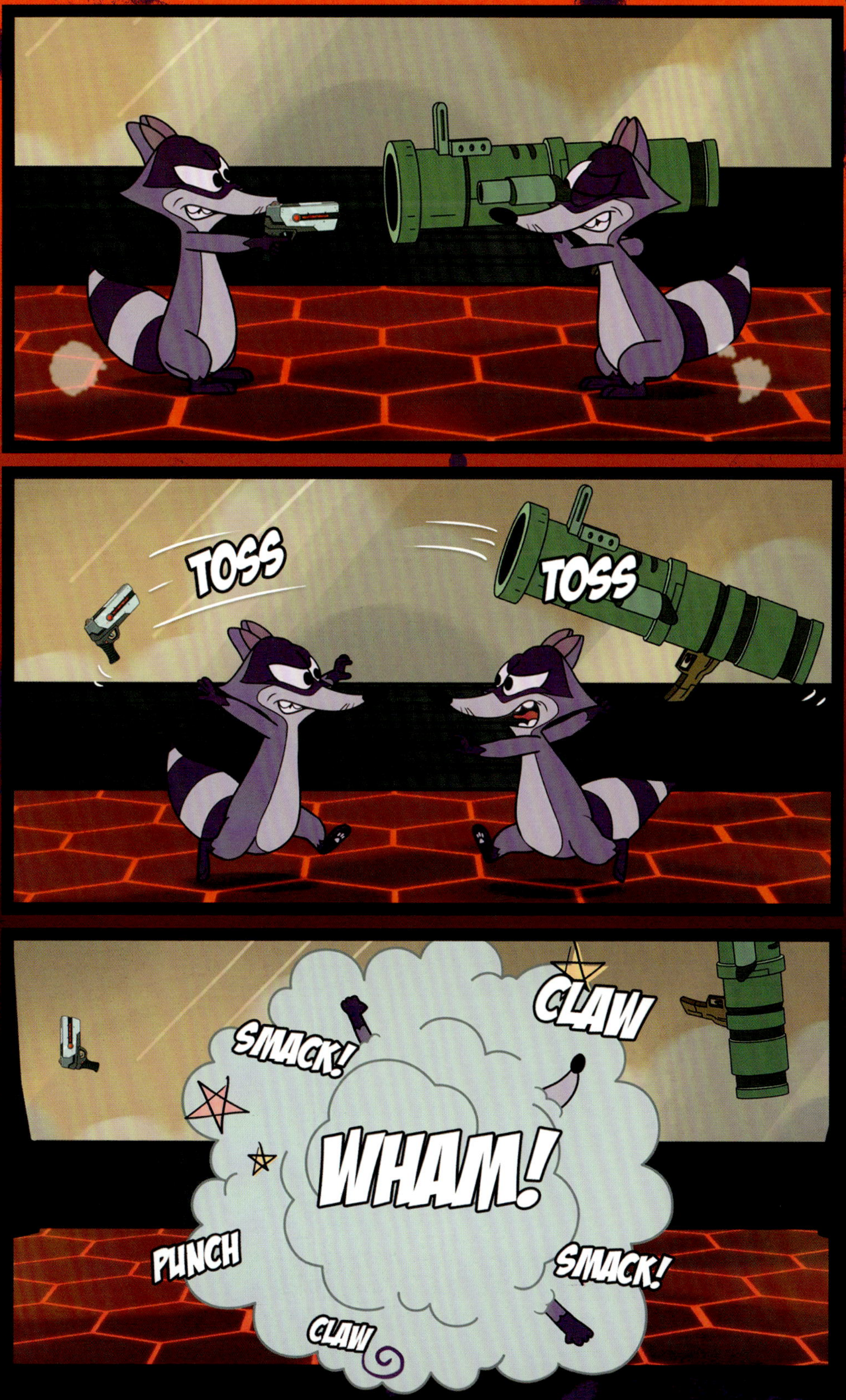
TOSS
TOSS
CLAW
SMACK!
WHAM!
PUNCH
SMACK!
CLAW

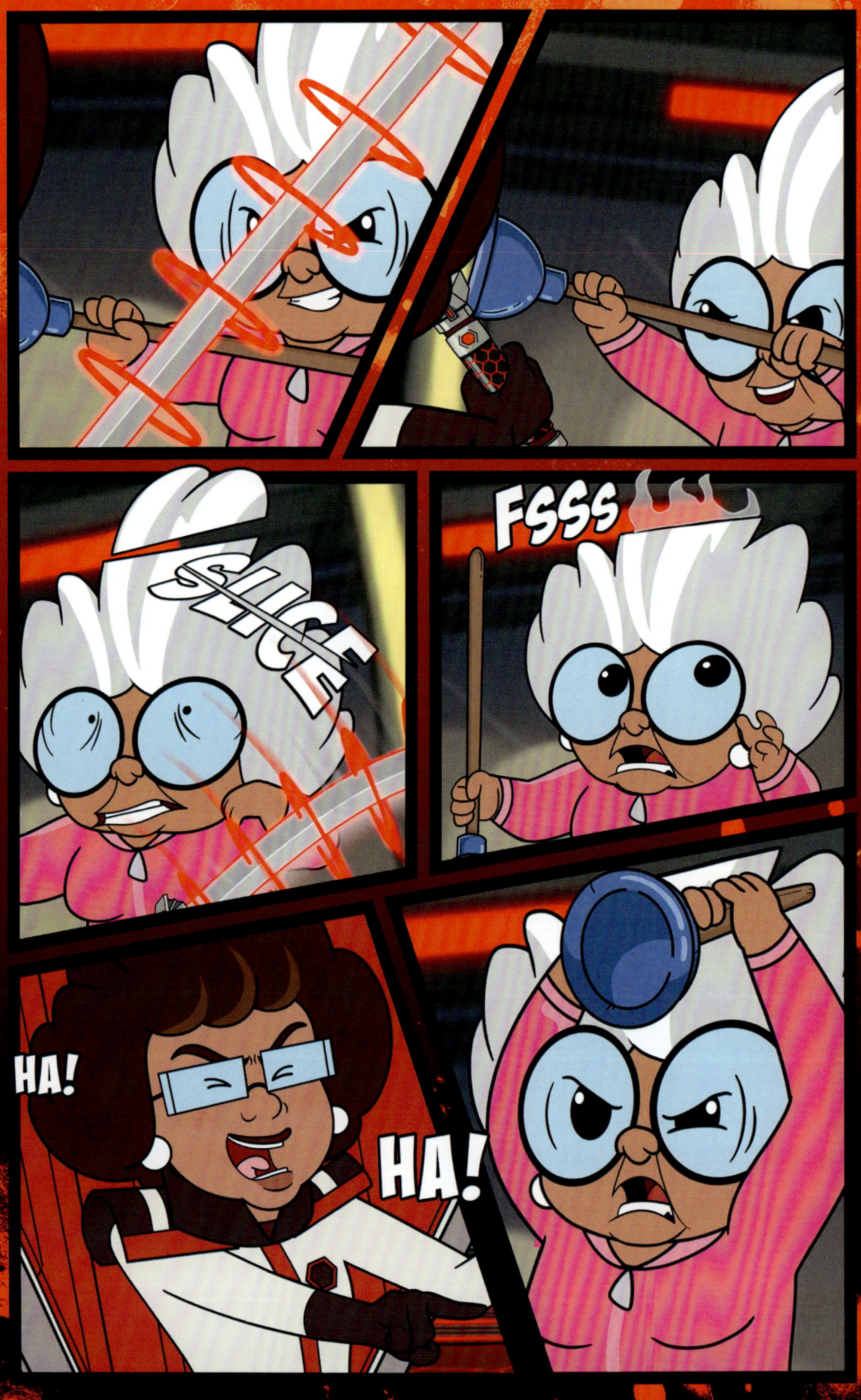
SLICE
FSSS
HA!
HA!

FUMP!

SO WHAT? WE SHOULD SURRENDER TO A FLAWED, UNEQUAL SYSTEM...

AND APPARENTLY COOKIES?

"LOOK. FREEDOM ISN'T PERFECT..."

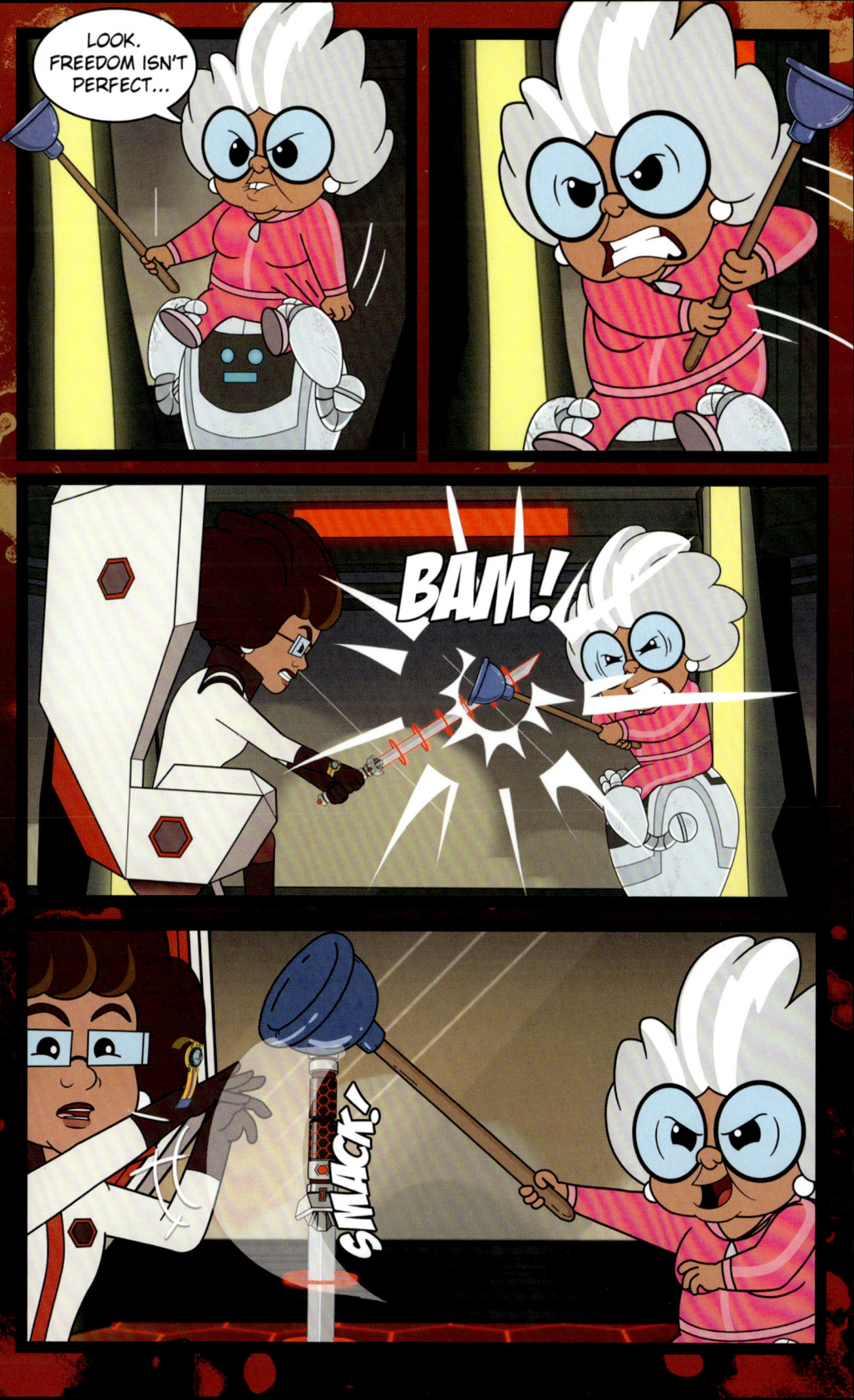

BAM!

SMACK!

BUT PERSUASION IS GREATER THAN FORCE.

THAT'S EASY FOR YOU TO SAY! THE SYSTEM HAS ALWAYS WORKED FOR YOU!
I AM YOU!
NO... NO!
IT'S NOT POSSIBLE! SO OLD, SO GORDA.
WOOSH
SEIZE HER!

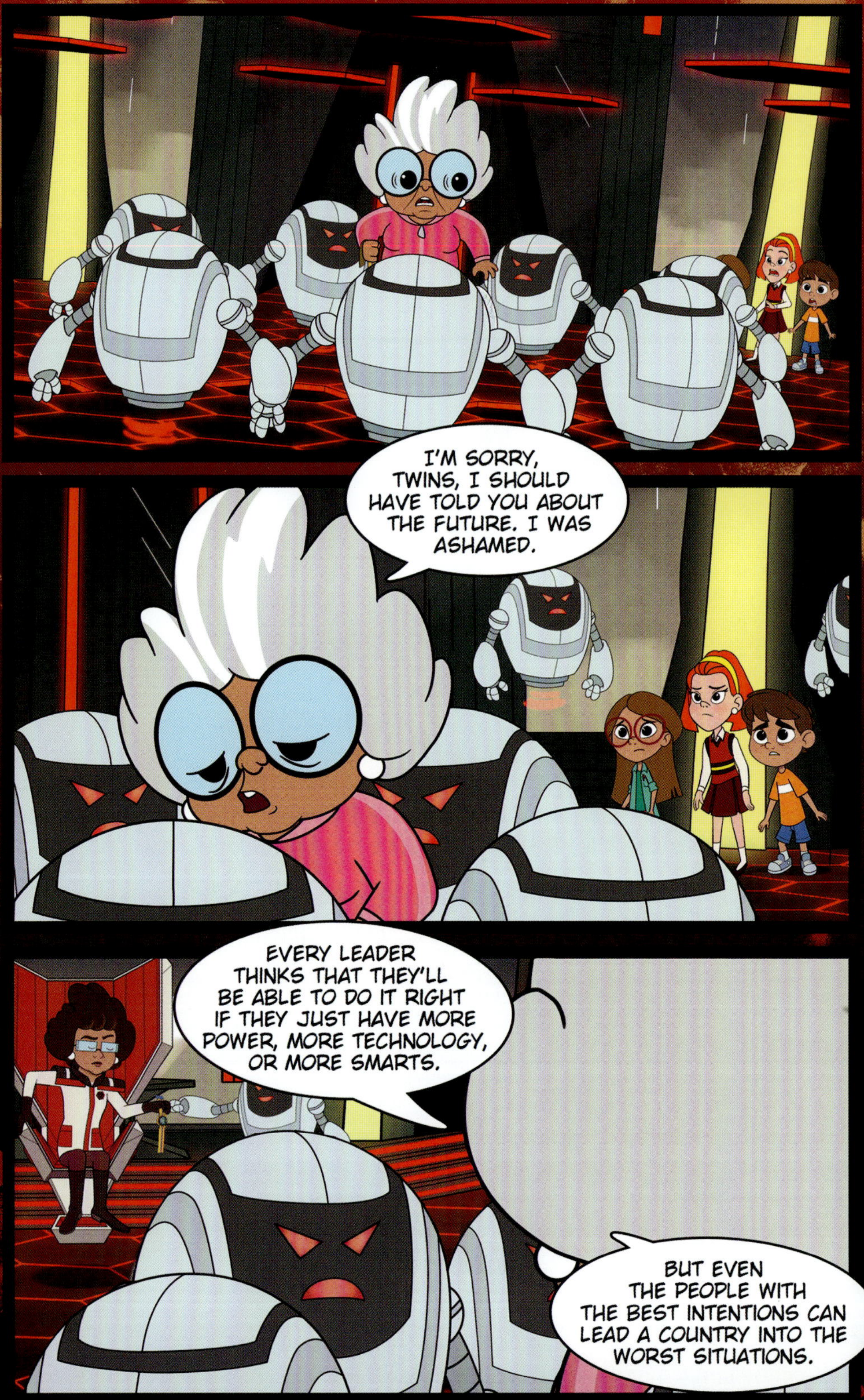
I'M SORRY, TWINS, I SHOULD HAVE TOLD YOU ABOUT THE FUTURE. I WAS ASHAMED.
EVERY LEADER THINKS THAT THEY'LL BE ABLE TO DO IT RIGHT IF THEY JUST HAVE MORE POWER, MORE TECHNOLOGY, OR MORE SMARTS.
BUT EVEN THE PEOPLE WITH THE BEST INTENTIONS CAN LEAD A COUNTRY INTO THE WORST SITUATIONS.

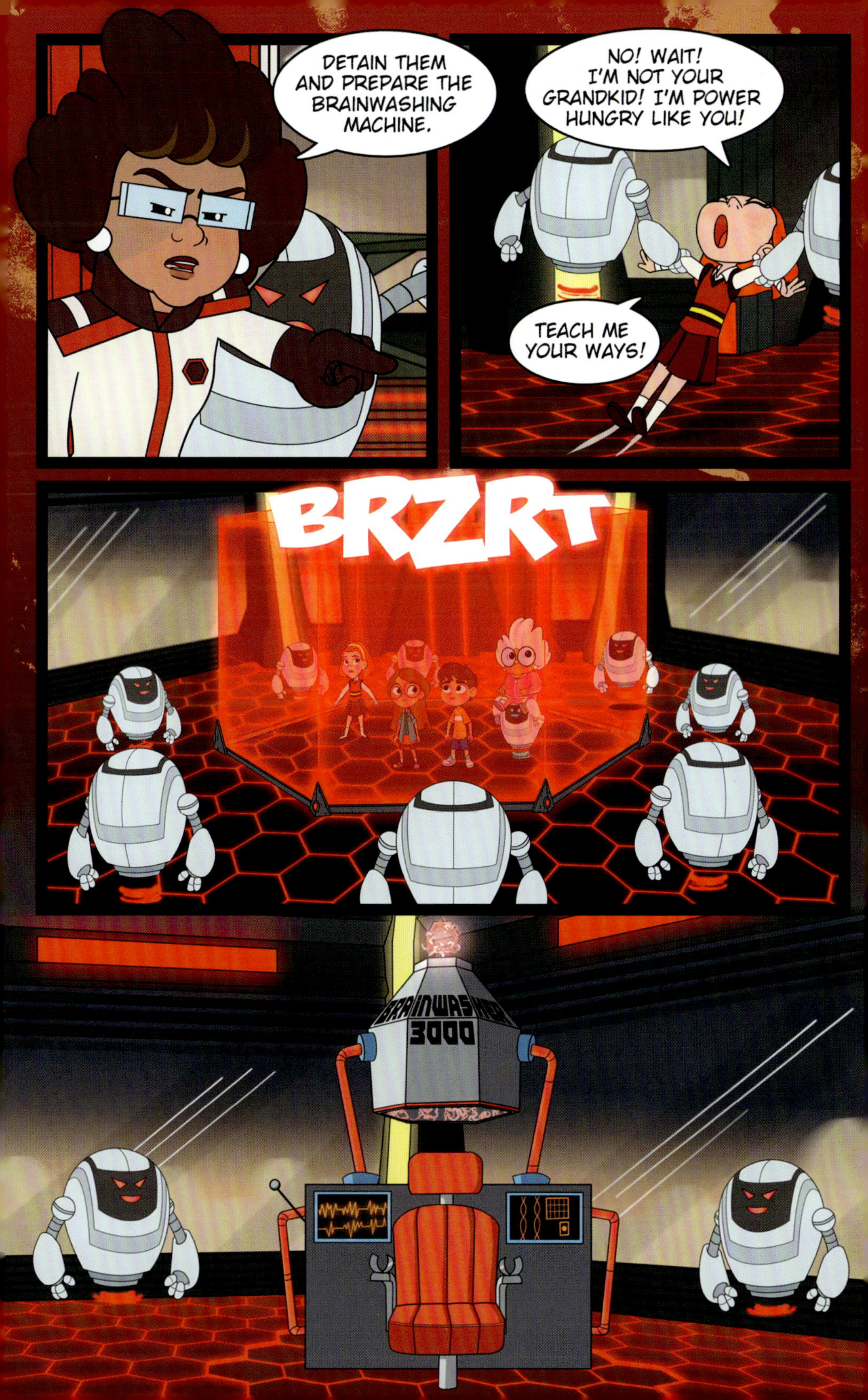
DETAIN THEM AND PREPARE THE BRAINWASHING MACHINE.
NO! WAIT! I'M NOT YOUR GRANDKID! I'M POWER HUNGRY LIKE YOU!
TEACH ME YOUR WAYS!
BRZRT
BRAINWASHER 3000

GABRIELA, THEY'RE YOUR GRANDKIDS TOO!
MIJOS, I HAVE FAILED YOU.
IN THE SENSE OF US BEING IMPRISONED AND POSSIBLY BRAINWASHED BY AN EVIL DICTATOR IN A FUTURISTIC JAIL? PROBABLY.

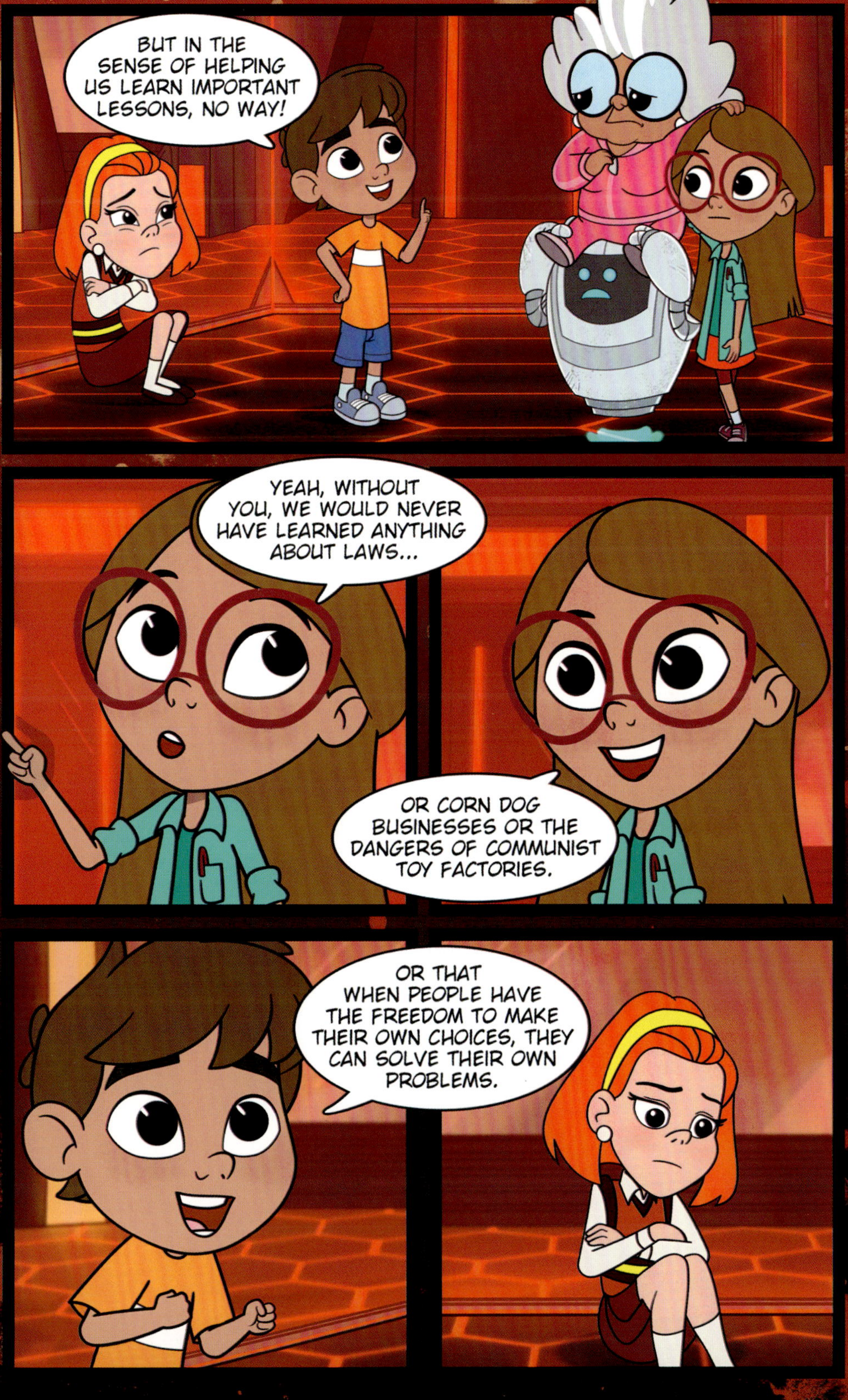
BUT IN THE SENSE OF HELPING US LEARN IMPORTANT LESSONS, NO WAY!
YEAH, WITHOUT YOU, WE WOULD NEVER HAVE LEARNED ANYTHING ABOUT LAWS...
OR CORN DOG BUSINESSES OR THE DANGERS OF COMMUNIST TOY FACTORIES.
OR THAT WHEN PEOPLE HAVE THE FREEDOM TO MAKE THEIR OWN CHOICES, THEY CAN SOLVE THEIR OWN PROBLEMS.

BUT WAIT. YOU DIDN'T STAY A TOTALITARIAN DICTATOR FOREVER. WHAT MADE YOU CHANGE?
YOU DID, AT THIS MOMENT.
I SAW MY ACTUAL FUTURE AND DECIDED TO RETURN TO THE PAST.

BLOOP
BLOOP
BRZRT
WELL, WOULD YOU LOOK AT THAT,
THE KNOWLEDGE JUICE IS FULL.

TOSS

VEET

VRRRT

OH, THANK GOODNESS!

I'M SO SORRY, MIJOS. I HAD NO IDEA THE FUTURE OF A FREE SOCIETY WAS SO BRIGHT... UNTIL I SAW YOU.
NO SWEAT, YOUNG GAB GAB.
YOU TURN OUT PRETTY GREAT IN THE END.

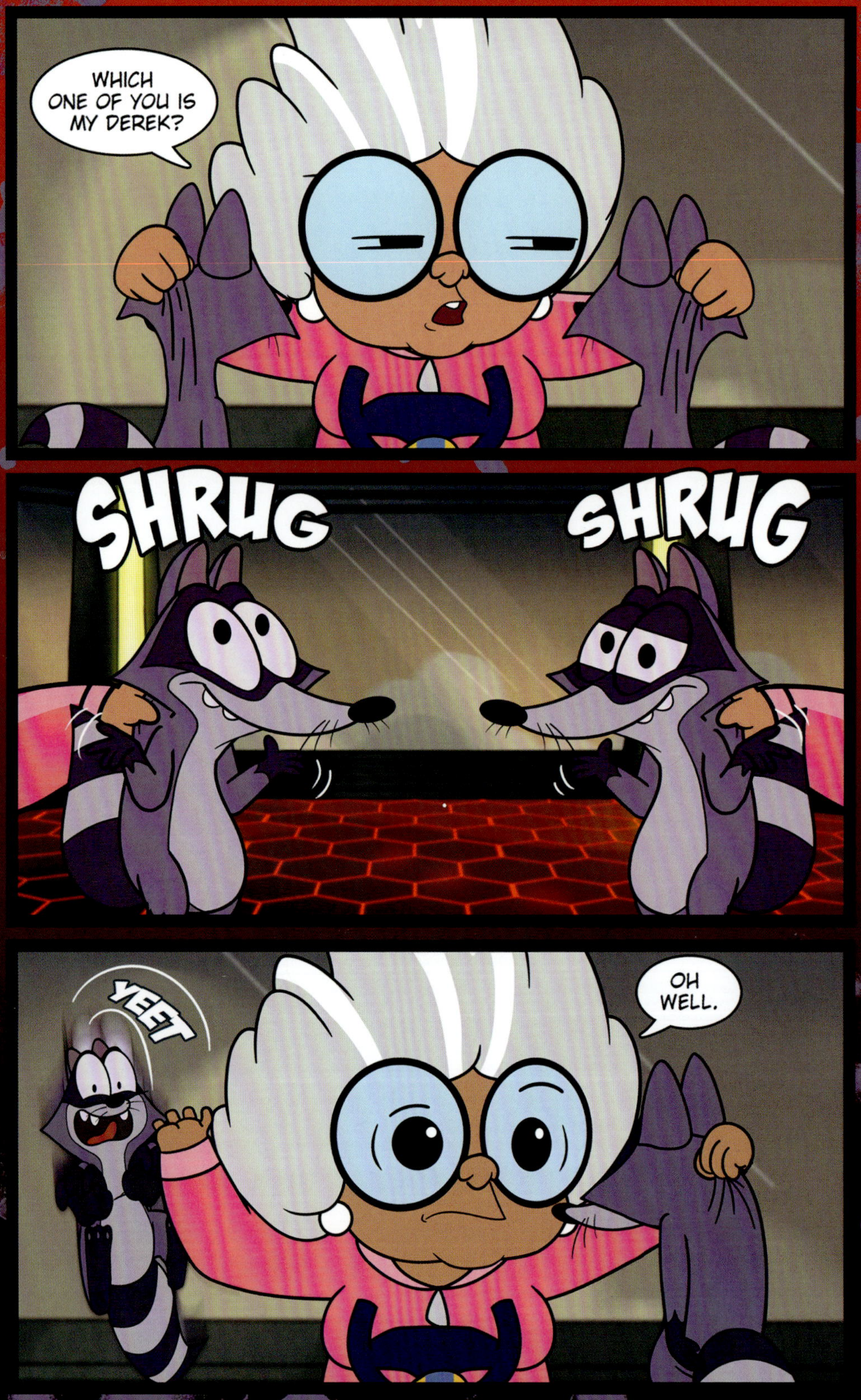
WHICH ONE OF YOU IS MY DEREK?
SHRUG
SHRUG
YEET
OH WELL.

SEE YOU IN 80 YEARS!
HOW OLD DO YOU THINK I AM?
SORRY. 90 YEARS!
UGH! WE STILL HAVE TO RIDE IN THIS STUPID TIME MACH-
AAHHH!!

PTSSS

SINCE WE ALREADY BROKE THE NO FUTURE RULE, LET ME SHOW YOU A FUTURE IN AN ALTERNATE DIMENSION THAT VALUES FREEDOM OVER FORCE.

DAVE'S PRIVATELY OWNED
DMV

NEW FOOT MASSAGE
MONDAYS

WELCOME TO DAVE'S PRIVATELY OWNED DMV. WE HAVE NO WAIT TIMES! ALSO, WE HAVE COOKIES!
DMV
OOOO!
:DROOLING EMOJI:
I LOST MY DRIVER'S LICENSE ON PURPOSE JUST SO I COULD COME AGAIN.
DMV
WE KNOW.
SEE? WHEN PEOPLE ARE GIVEN ACTUAL CHOICES, EVERYTHING IS BETTER.

FOLLOW YOUR PASSION ACADEMY
IMAGINE WHAT COULD HAPPEN IF YOU GOT TO CHOOSE THE SERVICES YOU USED.
LIKE SCHOOLS...
OUR SCHOOL HELPS YOUR KID FOLLOW THEIR PASSIONS, NOT STANDARDIZED CURRICULUMS!
POT HOLES FIXED IN A DAY OR YOUR MONEY BACK!
ROADS...
POT HOLE FIXER
CONSTRUCTION COMPLETE.
OR EVEN POLICE...
PEEDY POLICE
YOUR POLICE
WE DON'T INFRINGE ON YOUR RIGHTS!
WE'LL GET TO YOUR EMERGENCY IN 5 MINUTES OR LESS!
NO NO-KNOCK WARRANTS FOR US.

SO HOW DO WE GET TO THIS FUTURE?

BY GOING BACK IN TIME TO OUR DAY AND LIVING EVERYTHING YOU'VE LEARNED THIS SEASON.

THAT'S THE GREAT THING ABOUT THE FUTURE, IT DOESN'T HAVE TO TURN OUT LIKE THE ONE THAT MY YOUNGER, *BEAUTIFUL*, *PSYCHOTIC* SELF CREATED.

THE FATE OF THE FUTURE IS ALWAYS CHANGING, BASED ON OUR CHOICES NOW.

VRRRRRRR

BBBRRRRZZZTT!

BBBRRRZZZTT!

"WHY ARE WE HERE?"

"WELL, TECHNICALLY I'M STILL UNDER ARREST, PLUS DEREK HAS TO DO COMMUNITY SERVICE FOR ALL THE GOVERNMENT PROPERTY HE ATE."

"WELL, I GUESS... THANKS FOR SAVING MY LIFE OR WHATEVER, GRANDMA."

"YOU'RE WELCOME! AND NOW YOU OWE ME ONE LIFE SAVING FAVOR."

"UGH, I HATE THAT. BUT FINE."

"I'LL DELETE THOSE PICTURES OFF MY PHONE, BUT THEN WE'RE SQUARE. GOT IT?!"

"WOW, KARINNE. THAT'S REALLY BIG OF YOU."

"THAT, AND HER PHONE WAS LEFT IN THE FUTURE."

AH, KARINNE, YOU 'OL SOFTY. I THINK EVEN YOU LEARNED SOMETHING TODAY.
NO. WAY.
BUT, I **GUESS** I CAN SEE THAT THE YOUNG GRANDMA WANTED TO BE A GOOD LEADER, AND THAT SHE WASN'T VERY GOOD AT PERSUADING PEOPLE.
I LEARNED THAT ABSOLUTE POWER **CAN** CORRUPT-
EXCELLENT!
-THE WEAK WILLED.
THAT WOULD NEVER HAPPEN TO ME!

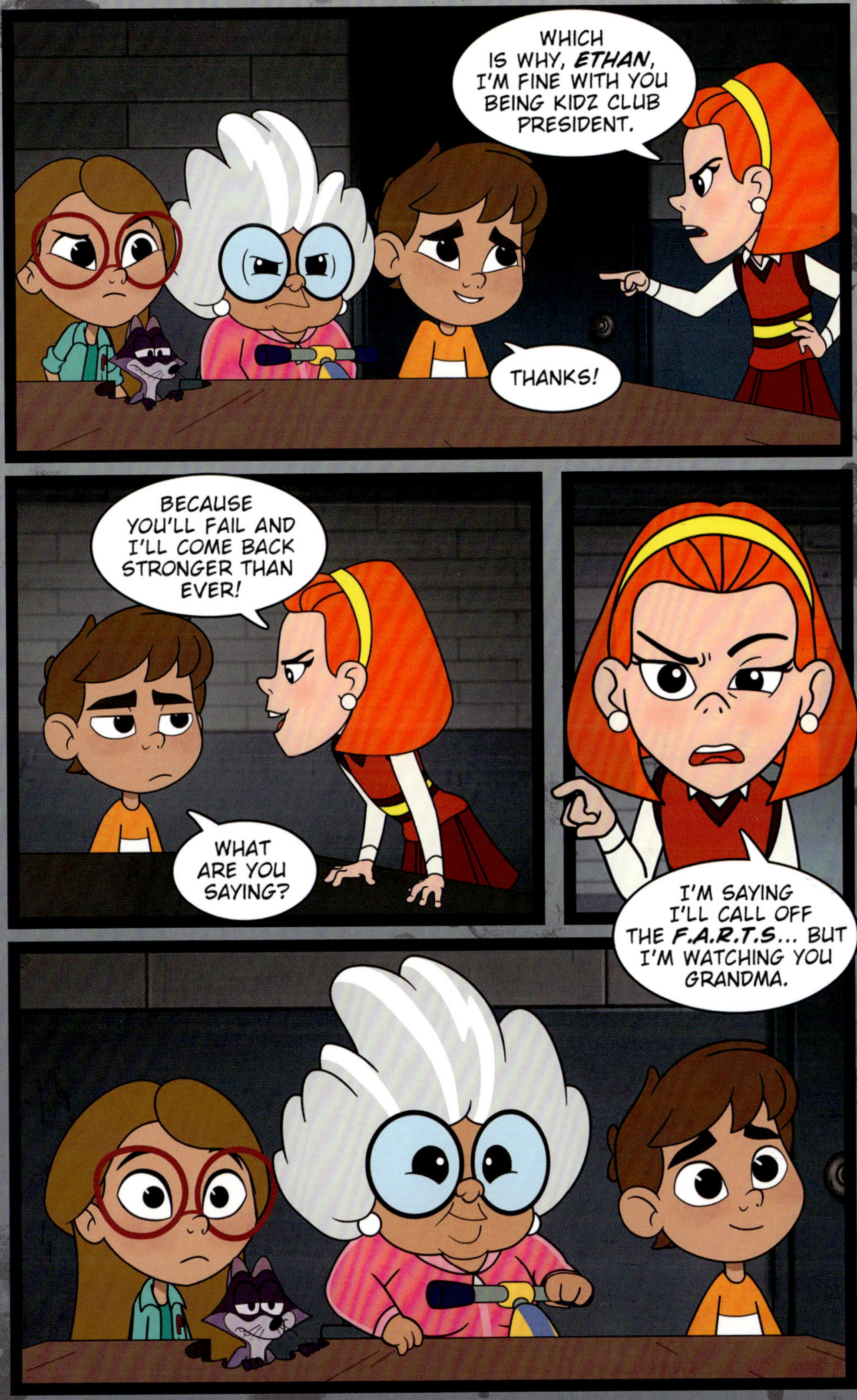
WHICH IS WHY, *ETHAN*, I'M FINE WITH YOU BEING KIDZ CLUB PRESIDENT.
THANKS!
BECAUSE YOU'LL FAIL AND I'LL COME BACK STRONGER THAN EVER!
WHAT ARE YOU SAYING?
I'M SAYING I'LL CALL OFF THE *F.A.R.T.S*... BUT I'M WATCHING YOU GRANDMA.

"GLAD YOU'RE ALL BACK."

"IF I COULD, I WOULD DEFINITELY LEAVE YOU A *1 STAR* REVIEW!"

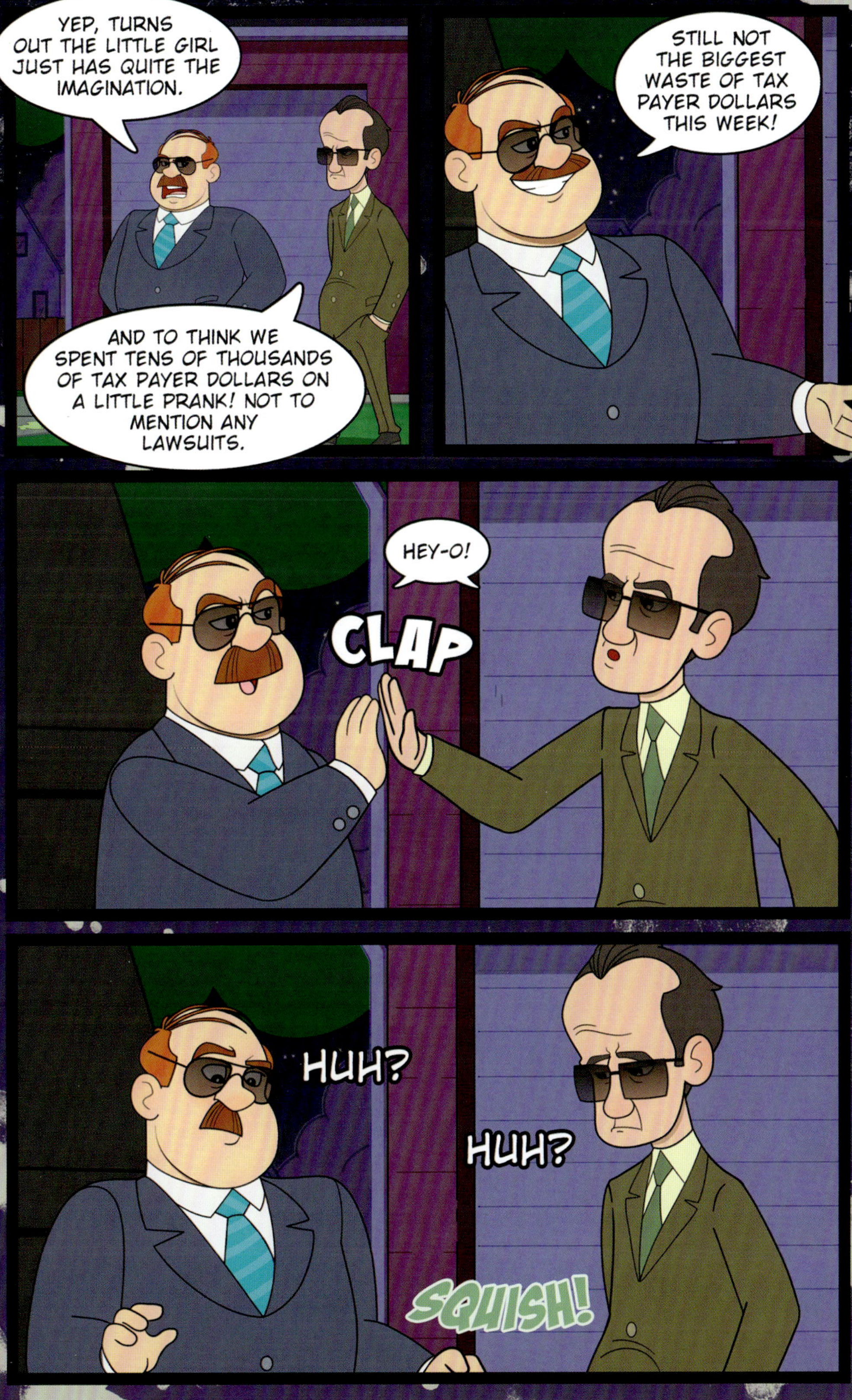
YEP, TURNS OUT THE LITTLE GIRL JUST HAS QUITE THE IMAGINATION.
AND TO THINK WE SPENT TENS OF THOUSANDS OF TAX PAYER DOLLARS ON A LITTLE PRANK! NOT TO MENTION ANY LAWSUITS.
STILL NOT THE BIGGEST WASTE OF TAX PAYER DOLLARS THIS WEEK!
HEY-O!
CLAP
HUH?
HUH?
SQUISH!

UGH, GRANDMA, YOUR WHEELCHAIR IS LEAKING KNOWLEDGE JUICE.

WHOOPS, I'LL NEED TO GET THAT FIXED!

HUH.

WHAT IS THAT?

I DON'T KNOW. BETTER TAKE THIS *UPSTAIRS.*

TO BE CONTINUED!

GET THE SEASON 2 NOVELS NOW!

BITCOIN AND THE BEAST
An Adventure About Hard Money

DON'T TRASH SUCCESS
An Adventure About Business Success

NEEDS, RIGHTS, & FLAMINGO FIGHTS
An Adventure About Needs vs Rights

12 MORE EXCITING ADVENTURES!

BUY IT NOW
TUTTLETWINS.STORE